6/23

EMILY POST'S
COMPLETE BOOK OF
WEDDING ETIQUETTE

REVISED EDITION

Also by Elizabeth L. Post

Emily Post's Etiquette, 14th Edition

Emily Post's Wedding Planner

Emily Post on Business Etiquette

Emily Post on Entertaining

Emily Post on Etiquette

Emily Post on Invitations and Letters

Emily Post on Second Weddings

Emily Post on Weddings

Emily Post Talks with Teens about Manners and Etiquette
(CO-AUTHOR JOAN M. COLES)

Emily Post's Complete Book of Entertaining
(WITH CO-AUTHOR ANTHONY STAFFIERI)

EMILY POST'S

COMPLETE BOOK OF

WEDDING ETIQUETTE

REVISED EDITION

ELIZABETH L. POST

HarperCollins*Publishers*

EMILY POST'S COMPLETE BOOK OF WEDDING ETIQUETTE, (*Revised Edition*). Copyright © 1991 by Elizabeth L. Post. All rights reserved. Printed in the United States of America. No part of this book may be used or reproduced in any manner whatsoever without written permission except in the case of brief quotations embodied in critical articles and reviews. For information address HarperCollins *Publishers,* 10 East 53rd Street, New York, New York 10022.

First Edition

Library of Congress Cataloging-in-Publication Data

Post, Elizabeth L.
    Emily Post's complete book of wedding etiquette / Elizabeth L.
Post. — Rev. ed.
    p.   cm.
    Includes index.
    ISBN 0-06-270006-5
    1. Wedding etiquette.   I. Post, Emily, 1873–1960.   II. Title.
III. Title: Complete book of wedding etiquette.
BJ2051.P54   1991
395'.22—dc20   90-55548

    93 94 95 CC/RRD 10 9 8 7 6

CONTENTS

1

THE ENGAGEMENT

R are today is the prospective bridegroom who drops to one knee and asks, "Will you marry me?" Increasingly, unmarried couples are living together before they feel they are ready for the commitment of marriage.

With the divorce rate in the United States hovering at 50 percent, previously married men and women have many decisions to make about their readiness to form a lasting union, and even young couples who are living at home with their parents or in apartments with roommates are more commonly deciding together to marry rather than leaving it to the future groom to "pop the question."

Whatever your situation, your mutual understanding has brought you to the point of planning to be married and there is much to discuss, both about your future life together and more immediately, about the form your wedding will take.

No matter what age the future bride and groom are, it is an unusual couple who don't want to share their happiness with the other people they love. Before marriage is even discussed, most men and women are anxious to introduce the person who has become so important to them to family members and even more anxious that they will get along and like one another.

Sharing the News

If you and your fiancé come from the same town it is likely that you know his parents, having visited them with him on different occasions as your relationship has progressed to one of closeness, and that he has gotten to know your parents as well. If your parents live some distance away, however, an overnight or weekend visit gives everyone a chance to meet before wedding bells are rung. Since your mother and father may have no idea that this is someone special in your life, you should give them a hint when making arrangements. The following notes would surely warn your parents that this visit is important to you and would diminish any chance of embarrassment to you or to your friend. Kate and Brian, who have not been married before, might write:

Dear Mom and Dad,

I've been spending a lot of time with a wonderful man, Brian Jamison, and I want you both to meet him. I'm sure you will like him as much as I know he will like you. I was wondering if we could both come for a visit on the 28th and 29th.

Please let me know as soon as you can.

Much love,
Kate

Brian would write:

Dear Mom,

I'm really looking forward to seeing you and wondered if it would be all right for me to bring Kate Adams with me. We have been seeing a lot of each other, and I want her to visit Minneapolis and to meet you. Let me know—

Love,
Brian

When you've been married before the situation is a little different. David and Susan, both of whom have grown children from previous marriages, would also want their families to meet this new and special person in their lives either by arranging a visit by or to their children. They would do this separately, however, making no plans to have each other's children meet at this point.

It is also important for Ben, who was married before and who has a young son and daughter, to make sure Beth is gradually included in some activities when his children visit him on weekends so that they have a chance to get used to one another and become friends before the word "marriage" is even mentioned.

If making plans to visit by telephone, Kate and Brian and David and Susan would be clear that while this is a special occasion and a special person, an engagement is still in the future.

Assuming that all goes well and that the courtship follows a normal course, the couples decide to get married and the rest of the world is let in on their secret. For Brian and Kate, their parents are the first to be told. It is up to the couple whether each wishes to tell his or her own mother and father privately or whether they go together to break the news. If the families are far away, Brian and Kate telephone or write their own parents.

Although it may seem old-fashioned, it is still courteous for the prospective groom to explain his plans and his prospects to the bride's parents. Today this conversation is usually carried out with the bride present. However it is arranged, this discussion is an important evidence of the groom's respect for the bride's parents and a courtesy that should not be neglected.

David and Susan would first call their children to share their happy news, each calling his or her own children. It would be hoped that David's children, in turn, would speak to Susan and express their happiness and that Susan's children would do the same with David.

Ben should tell his son and daughter of his plans without Beth present to give them time to adjust to the idea and should talk to them again, with Beth, who can tell them how she feels. Ben should then tell his ex-wife that he plans to be married again and that the children have been told. If his children are initially anxious about this marriage or feel threatened in any way, he should reassure them that his love for them is not being taken away and given to Beth, although he loves her very much. Once the children have adjusted to the idea of their father's remarriage, both he and Beth should include them as much as is possible in wedding plans so that they do not feel left out. If the children are not happy about the marriage, however, they should not be forced to participate in the ceremony.

When Families Aren't Supportive

Should Kate's parents indicate that they disapprove of the marriage, she faces a difficult decision. Either she accedes to her parents' wishes or she determines to marry despite their disapproval. If she chooses the latter course, she should inform them when her wedding will take place and tell them that it would make her very happy if they would attend. In no case should she give her word that she will not marry while intending to do so. The same would hold true should Brian's mother disapprove of Kate.

Fortunately, however, this is not generally the case. If Kate's parents feel that she and Brian have a reasonable prospect of supporting themselves, believe that they are suited to each other in interests and personalities, and approve of Brian as a person, they give their approval at once.

When the couple has grown children, as David and Susan do, other elements enter into the picture. Certainly David and Susan do not need their childrens' permission to marry. But they do hope to have their childrens' support and best wishes. These children, although adults, may be concerned about the impact of their parents remarriage on their lives, unsettled by the prospect of someone replacing a deceased parent, or unsure of the implications for their financial future, or any number of other individual concerns. Whatever the reason, each of these concerns needs to be addressed in an open and honest way. Initially, the adult children may not be comfortable discussing their feelings with their future stepparent present, so both David and Susan make time to meet with their children privately to listen to their concerns. Should the childrens' concern be about financial matters it is especially important that these be discussed openly allowing the parent to assure them that their interests will be protected.

After some initial hesitancy on their part, Susan's children aired their feelings to her, and later to her and David together, in a frank and forthright manner. While this conversation was not an easy one to have it served to clear the air and reassure everyone involved. Susan and David may now plan their wedding with the love and support of their families.

The Families Meet

As soon as Brian has talked to the Adamses, Brian's mother should get in touch with Mrs. Adams. Years ago the man's parents made a formal call on those of the young woman, often arriving unannounced, calling cards in hand, at the door. Today, Mrs. Jamison telephones Mrs. Adams, tells her how happy she is about the engagement, and suggests that they get together. She may invite the Adamses for cocktails, for dinner, or for an after-dinner coffee. Or she may ask Mrs. Adams to suggest a convenient time when she may drop in. If Kate were not nearby and had not met her future mother-in-law, Mrs. Jamison would immediately write her future daughter-in-law a letter welcoming her into the family. Since the parents live in different areas, Mrs. Jamison asks the Adamses to visit. If this is impractical or difficult the Adamses should feel free to explain and ask that Mrs. Jamison visit them instead. If it seems impossible for the two families to meet at this time, they should correspond or talk on the telephone and look forward to meeting at the first wedding festivities.

Brian's mother is a widow, but when the parents of one or both members of the bridal couple are divorced, getting the families together is a little more complicated. But generally speaking, the parent with whom the groom has been living, or with whom he lived after the divorce, is the one who makes the first move. If the bride's parents are divorced, it is the one with whom she lived (or is living) who is invited first to the groom's parents' home. However, the other parent, if he or she is still close to the bride, should be invited very shortly thereafter.

Whatever arrangements are made, it is the groom's family who should make the initial move. But even more important is the necessity that the two families do get together. If for one reason or another Mrs. Jamison does not realize this, or does not know how to go about it, Kate's parents should quickly take the initiative. It would be most unfortunate to start off with ill feeling between the families because of a misunderstanding. This time should be a happy one and both sets of parents should act enthusiastically and in a spirit of friendship.

At the same time it is essential that Kate and Brian try to understand the attitudes of their future in-laws. They must take care not to insist on standing inflexibly on what they may consider their rights. The objective to keep in mind is the ultimate happiness of their relationships with each other's family.

It is not essential for David's or Susan's children to attempt a meeting, or those of any other older couple, since it is unlikely that their lives will intertwine to the extent that Kate's and Brian's parents will, although David and Susan may arrange a meeting of their families if it is important to them to do so.

Ben's and Beth's parents would follow the same protocol as Kate's and Brian's parents, even though Ben has been married before.

Once their family has been told, the engaged couples are free to tell as many friends and relatives as they wish of their engagement. Or they may prefer to keep it a secret until the formal announcement. In any case, a few days or weeks before the news appears in the paper or an engagement party is held, relatives and close friends should be informed in person, by telephone, or by note—to prevent hurt feelings.

The Engagement Ring

An engagement ring is not essential to becoming engaged. Many young couples prefer to put the money that would be spent on it to more practical uses, such as a longer honeymoon or furnishings for their home. However, most young men want to show their love by giving their future bride the most beautiful ring they can afford.

The days when a man pulled a ring from his pocket the moment a woman said yes are gone forever. Today, it is both correct and wise for him to consult her before buying the ring. One method is for Brian to go to a jeweler, explain what he wants and how much he can afford, and have a selection of rings set aside. Then he takes Kate to the store, and she chooses the one she likes best. Or she may simply make a selection, and they decide together whether the cost is reasonable.

A diamond is still the usual choice, although colored stones have become much more popular in recent years. Some brides prefer a large semiprecious stone, such as an amethyst or an aquamarine, rather than a much smaller diamond. Others choose their birthstone, or that of the groom. If the bridegroom is fortunate enough to have a family heirloom to give his bride, she may, if she wishes, go with him to select a new setting.

For those brides who choose a birthstone:

January — *Garnet or zircon*
February — *Amethyst*
March — *Aquamarine or bloodstone*
April — *Diamond*
May — *Emerald*
June — *Pearl*
July — *Ruby*
August — *Sardonyx or carnelian*
September — *Sapphire*
October — *Opal, moonstone*
November — *Topaz*
December — *Turquoise, lapis lazuli*

Kate first wears her engagement ring in public on the day of the official announcement. If no official announcement is going to be made, Kate may wear her ring as soon as she receives it. If Brian could not afford a ring at the time of the engagement, he might give her one at any time later—when he feels he can buy her the ring he has always wanted her to have.

It is a good idea for the bride and groom to select a wedding ring at the same time that they choose her engagement ring. The two rings are often purchased as a matching set, although this is not necessary. The band of the engagement ring is almost always made of gold or platinum, and the wedding ring should be of the same element. If it is to be a double-ring ceremony, the bride should choose the groom's ring at the same time so that they will be well matched. The groom's ring is generally similar to, but somewhat heavier than, the bride's. The wedding rings often bear an inscription inside, most commonly the couple's initials and the date of the wedding.

The Engagement Party

Once the bride's parents have met her fiancé's family and the ring has been purchased, it is time to make the engagement official. If you, like Kate and Brian, plan to have an engagement party, it is up to your mother and father—with your assistance—to give it. However, if your own parents live far away, there is no reason that your fiancé's mother and father shouldn't give the party if they wish to. The one requirement is that both you and your fiancé be present. If he is overseas with the armed forces or absent for any other reason, you may announce the engagement in the paper, but you must wait for his return to hold the party.

David's and Susan's adult children could honor them with an engagement party if they live nearby, which would be a lovely way to show their support of their parents' plans, and Beth's parents would make plans similar to those of Kate's parents. If Beth and not Ben had been married before, she might forgo an engagement party and simply tell close friends and relatives by note or telephone call, although an engagement party would not be improper.

Invitations are generally sent out in the name of your parents. They need not mention the reason for the party, especially if you are trying to make it a surprise. This is rarely successful, however, and more often the nature of the occasion is made clear on the invitation. If the invitation is printed, or when the wording is formal, "In honor of Katherine Adams and Brian Jamison" is written by hand at the top.

It is also perfectly correct to issue the invitations by an informal handwritten note or by telephone.

There are innumerable ways of breaking the news at the party, and your own good taste and imagination may provide a novel and interesting idea. Since your mother, you, and your fiancé should be standing at the door to greet the guests, there is really little need for any announcement at all. But cocktail napkins printed with your name and your fiancé's name, or place cards in the form of a telegram announcing the news, make attractive mementos of the occasion for guests who may be scrapbook enthusiasts.

Toasts

Mr. Adams makes the engagement official by proposing a toast to the bride. Since the Adamses have chosen to give a cocktail party, he may do this as soon as all the guests have arrived and have their drinks. If it were a dinner party, he would wait until everyone were seated or, if he preferred, until dessert were served. His toast may be the very briefest: "Will you all join me in a toast to Kate and Brian." Or, if he wishes to be more eloquent, he might say something like this:

"Please drink with me to the happiness of the couple who are so close to our hearts—Kate and Brian."

"I'd like to propose a toast to the health of Kate and the newest member of our family—Brian."

Everyone except Kate and Brian rises and drinks a little of the beverage in front of them. Brian, at this point, should reply to Kate's father's toast. If he is shy and inarticulate, all he need say is, "Kate and I want to thank you all for being here, and for your good wishes." If he is more of an extrovert, he may add a remark or two.

"I don't have to tell you all how lucky I am. I do have to prove, if I can, that Kate hasn't made the mistake of her life in choosing me."

"My debt to the Adamses is twofold—first for having brought Kate into the world, and second for entrusting her to me."

It is not necessary for other members of the party to propose toasts, but it is perfectly proper if they wish to do so.

Gifts

The bride-to-be does not necessarily give her fiancé an engagement present, but you may certainly do so if you wish. The gift is usually jewelry—initialed belt buckle or cuff links, a key chain, or a watch. Engagement gifts are not expected from ordinary friends and acquaintances. They are given only by relatives and very special friends and are usually given to the bride alone. Such a gift is personal—lingerie or jewelry, perhaps. Or it may be something for her linen trousseau—towels, a blanket cover, table linen, a comforter, or a decorative pillow. If the presents are monogrammed, most brides today prefer that they be marked with their married initials. Presents should not be given at an engagement party. Since only close relatives and friends give gifts, it could cause embarrassment to those who have not brought anything.

If the gifts are delivered to you in person and you thank the givers sincerely at the time, you need do nothing more. If any are sent to your home, or left there in your absence, you should write a note of thanks immediately. You should also write notes promptly in response to all welcoming or congratulatory messages that you receive.

Announcing the Engagement

An engagement may be made public through a newspaper announcement. It is not in good taste to send engraved or printed announcements. The article usually appears in the newspaper two or three months before the proposed date of the marriage, although the wedding plans need not have been completed. If the circumstances warrant, the announcement may appear up to a year before the wedding date, or as little as a week ahead. Announcements may be put in the paper by any couple who wish to be sure that all their acquaintances know of their happiness. Widows and divorcées, in some cases, may prefer to make their news known privately, and that is perfectly correct; it is entirely up to them.

The only time a public announcement is not in good taste is when there has recently been a death in either family, or if a member of the immediate family is desperately ill. In these cases the news is spread by word of mouth, although a public announcement may follow some weeks later.

The announcement of the engagement is generally made by the bride's parents or her immediate family. The information should be clearly written out and sent to large city newspapers three weeks or more ahead of the date you wish it to appear. In local newspapers a week or ten days is usually sufficient. The letter is addressed to the society editor or the society news department of the paper. Be sure to include telephone numbers in your letter so that the information can be verified. The bride's family should ask the parents of the groom if they would like to have the announcement appear in their locality. If the groom's family says yes, the bride's mother should send the same announcement to the papers they specify. If the bride's parents do not suggest this, it is quite proper for the groom's mother to put the announcement in her local papers—*in the name of the bride's parents.* If either family wishes to have a picture appear, a glossy black-and-white print must accompany the written information. This picture used to be of the bride alone, but today it may also be a picture of the couple. The date on which you would like the news to be published should be given to all the newspapers at the same time so that the notices will appear simultaneously.

Although each newspaper has its own special wording, the information included and the general form will be as follows:

Mr. and Mrs. Howard Adams of Briarcliff Manor, New York, announce the engagement of their daughter, Miss Katherine Leigh Adams, to Mr. Brian Charles Jamison, son of Mrs. Richard Jamison of Minneapolis, Minnesota, and the late Mr. Jamison. A June wedding is planned.

Miss Adams was graduated from New York University and is a communications assistant for the National Broadcasting Company. Mr. Jamison was graduated from the University of Minnesota. He is at present associated with Moore Associates advertising agency in New York City.

Although the identification of the bride and groom and their parents may vary, the information as to schools and employment remains the same. Following are some situations that require different wording in the announcement:

When one of the bride's parents is deceased: The announcement is worded the same whether made by the mother or the father of the bride.

Mrs. [Mr.] Allan Robert Rogers announces the engagement of her [his] daughter, Miss Joanne Lynn Rogers, to Dr. William Kelly . . . etc. Miss Rogers is also the daughter of the late Allan Robert [Joyce Green] Rogers . . .

If a parent of the groom is deceased:

Mr. and Mrs. Mark Steglitz announce the engagement of their daughter, Miss Sandra Steglitz, to Mr. John Williams, son of Mrs. Adam Carter Williams and the late Mr. Williams . . .

If the parents are divorced: The mother of the bride usually makes the announcement, but, as in the case of a deceased parent, the name of the other parent must be included:

Mrs. Lucinda Castronova announces the engagement of her daughter, Miss Valerie Castronova . . . Miss Castronova is also the daughter of Mr. Julio Castronova of Worcester, Massachusetts . . .

If divorced parents are friendly: On occasion, divorced parents may remain good friends, and their daughter's time may be divided equally between them. If this is true, they may both wish to announce the engagement:

Mr. James Gibson of Philadelphia and Mrs. Christopher Morris of Palm Beach, Florida, announce the engagement of their daughter, Miss Carla Gibson . . .

If the parent with whom the bride lives is remarried:

Mr. and Mrs. Douglas Skolnick announce the engagement of Mrs. Skolnick's daughter, Miss Marcy Rectenwald, to . . . Miss Rectenwald is also the daughter of Mr. Franklin Scott Rectenwald of Lake Tahoe, Nevada . . .

If the bride is adopted: If the bride has been brought up with the family since she was an infant and has the same name as her adoptive parents, there is no reason to mention the fact that she is adopted. If she joined the family later in life, however, and has retained her own name, it is proper to say:

Mr. and Mrs. Abbott Smythe announce the engagement of their adopted daughter, Miss Karen Reardon, daughter of the late Mr. and Mrs. Carlton Reardon . . .

When the bride is an orphan: The engagement of an orphan is announced by her nearest relative, a godparent, or a very dear friend. She may also announce her own engagement, impersonally:

The engagement of Miss Maryann Hayes (daughter of the late Mr. and Mrs. Samuel Hayes) is announced, to Mr. Jay Pomranze . . .

When the bride is a widow: The parents of a young widow would announce her engagement in the same way as they did the first time she was married, using her current name:

Mr. and Mrs. Allan Wheat announce the engagement of their daughter, Mrs. Jasper Fountain [or Anne Wheat Fountain] . . .

When the bride is a divorcée: The parents of a young divorcée would announce her engagement as would the parents of a young widow, using her former husband's last name if she continues to use his name, or her maiden name if she has changed her name back following a divorce:

Mr. and Mrs. Thomas Hauranek announce the engagement of their daughter, Mrs. Amanda Bieler [or Amanda Hauranek Bieler] [or Amanda Sue Hauranek] to . . .

Older women: An older woman, whether marrying for the first time or a divorcée or widow, may announce her own engagement, or may forgo a newspaper announcement and notify friends and relatives by note or telephone. If she chooses to announce her engagement in the newspaper:

The engagement of Miss [or Mrs.] Diana Trainer to Mr. Salvator Iannuzzi has been announced . . .

When the groom's parents announce the engagement: Occasionally a situation arises in which the parents of the groom would like to announce the engagement. For instance, when a man in the service becomes engaged to a girl from another country, her parents may not have the knowledge or means to put an announcement in the paper in his home town. Rather than announce it in their own name, the groom's parents should word the notice:

The engagement of Miss Inger Strauss, daughter of Mr. and Mrs. Heinrich Strauss of Munich, Germany, to Lt. John Evans, son of Mr. and Mrs. Walter Evans of Chicago, is announced.

When there has been a recent death in either family, the announcement may be put in the newspaper later, and a big engagement party is not held.

No announcement should *ever* be made of an engagement in which either person is still legally married to someone else—no matter how close the divorce or annulment may be.

Timing

Whether the newspaper announcement appears before or after the engagement party is a matter of the couple's choice and local custom. If they wish to surprise their guests, naturally the party is held the day before the news appears in the paper. However, it is equally correct to have the party follow the announcement, right away or even days or weeks later.

If an engagement is broken, the bride must immediately return the ring, and all other presents of any value her fiancé has given her. Engagement gifts given her by both families should also be returned, as well as those sent by friends. The bride who is embarrassed to deliver them in person should send them by mail, accompanied by an explanatory note:

Dear Ginny,

I am sorry to have to tell you that Jim and I have broken our engagement. Therefore, I am returning the towels that you were kind enough to send me.

Love,
Sara

If the engagement was announced in the paper, a notice should appear announcing that the marriage will not take place. This will allay embarrassing questions such as "When is the wedding?" as well as letting all who are interested know what has happened. The notice need say no more than "The engagement of Miss Sara Brown and Mr. James Forster has been broken by mutual consent."

Should the man die before the wedding takes place, the woman may keep her engagement ring. If it is a family heirloom, however, and she suspects that his parents would like to keep it in the family, she would be considerate to offer to return it. She may keep gifts given by relatives and friends if she wishes. But she may well prefer to return them rather than have them about as constant reminders of this tragedy.

The Length of the Engagement

The ideal length of an engagement is between three and six months. This allows ample time for the couple to make wedding arrangements and to find and perhaps furnish their future home. When longer than that, an engagement may get to be involved. If a man is overseas in the armed forces, or if one of the couple is still in college and far away, they may wish to announce their engagement so that they may easily avoid going out with other men or women. But when they are together for an extended period, the pressures of trying to see each other as much as possible and at the same time carry on their work or studies may become very serious. In addition to her normal routine, the bride often has the time-consuming responsibilities of planning their wedding. Therefore, unless there are excellent reasons for a long engagement, a short one more probably ensures that the bride, the groom, and their families will arrive at the wedding in good health and in a happy frame of mind.

The Behavior of the Couple

Of course, all the world loves a lover, but the most attractive way for a couple to show their affection is by open approval of each other's actions, not by public physical displays.

Engaged men and women should not show an interest in *a particular member* of the opposite sex. If they are separated, they need not sit home alone, but neither should they have "twosome" dates. They should not see the same person frequently or let an occasional meeting lead to others of a more intimate nature.

During this period, it is most important that you do not avoid the company of others. Naturally you will want to spend a great deal of time alone together, and those hours will be your favorite ones, but it is essential that you get to know each other's friends. When one member of a couple is incompatible with those who have been a part of the other's life, the marriage has one strike against it at the start.

What Should You Call Your Fiancé's Parents?

During the engagement period, the bride-to-be may, if she does not know them well, continue to refer to her future in-laws formally. For example, Kate calls Brian's mother "Mrs. Jamison." If she has known her for many years and is accustomed to calling her by a nickname, or possibly "Aunt," she should go on using those terms. Otherwise, as she becomes closer to her, she might shorten the formal "Mrs. Jamison" to "Mrs. J." If Mrs. Jamison wishes Kate to use her first name or nickname, and specifically requests her to do so, she should, of course, comply. This generally is done at some point after the wedding, if she has not already started to use a derivative of "Mother." Preferably she chooses a name other than that which she uses for her own mother.

This question of names is a truly sensitive one, and thoughtfulness must be observed on both sides. If a nickname does not come about naturally, or if the woman does not wish to use names that her husband-to-be uses for his parents, tact is required to avoid too much formality—or too little respect. The best solution is an open discussion. Kate and Brian may ask Mrs. Jamison quite frankly what she would like Kate to call her, or Mrs. Jamison may make a suggestion herself. The same procedure should be followed by Brian with Kate's parents.

If it seems too difficult a subject to bring up and a solution does not happen naturally, the safest compromise is the one mentioned—"Mrs. J." by Kate to Brian's mother, and "Mr. and Mrs. A." by Brian to Kate's parents.

2

THE BRIDE'S TROUSSEAU

Traditionally, the articles a future bride or her mother made or embroidered for use after her marriage were kept in a hope chest. Today, few articles are handmade, and there is no need to start years ahead amassing things that can be purchased in a few hours' time. Therefore a chest is more often acquired after the engagement is announced and used to put away the gifts and the purchases made by the bride or her mother for her trousseau. Today the hope chest often takes the form of a chest of drawers to be used later in the bride's new home.

The Bride's Personal Trousseau

A trousseau, according to the derivation of the word, was the "little trusse" or "bundle" that the bride carried with her to the house of her husband. The dozens of frilly pieces of lingerie and lacy table linens that were once considered indispensable have been replaced by articles that are regarded as necessary by our modern standards.

There is no rule about how many pieces of lingerie or what kinds of clothes a bride should have in her personal trousseau. It depends entirely on her financial situation and the life that she and her groom will be leading. She should, however, plan to begin her marriage with a wardrobe sufficient to last her for one season, and preferably for one year. A bride need not feel that her wardrobe must consist entirely of new things; she should keep all of her old clothing that she particularly likes, as long as it is in serviceable condition. The three new articles that every bride should have if she can possibly afford them are her wedding dress, her going-away costume, and a nightgown and negligee for her honeymoon.

The Household Trousseau

While it is impossible to itemize the bride's personal clothes, it is quite possible to make practical suggestions for household necessities. The lists below include minimum amounts of linen, china, crystal, and silver for the young bride who will live in a small house or apartment. Even though she may be able to afford larger quantities, she should remember that closet and storage space will undoubtedly be very limited until she and her husband can have a larger home. Naturally the bride who starts out with bigger quarters, and expects to entertain on a larger scale, must add to these lists whatever she feels will be necessary.

Unlike many younger couples, David and Susan very likely have doubles of household items, since both are entering this marriage from their own homes and after years of accumulating items during their previous marriages. They will want to consolidate and will have to make decisions about whose china or flatware, for example, they will use, or whether they wish to give away or sell what they already own and make a fresh start with new items. For them, these lists are a guideline for checking among their possessions to make sure that what they already own is in good repair and for determining what else they might need.

Bed Linen

4 sheets for master bed (or, if master beds are twin size, 4 for each)
4 sheets for each single bed
2 pillowcases for each single bed
2 quilted mattress pads for each bed
1 lightweight blanket for each bed
1 electric blanket, or 2 woolen blankets and 1 comforter for each bed
1 bedspread for each bed (unless guest beds are convertible sofas)
  extra pillows for guests
  Optional:
1 blanket cover for master bed, preferably permanent press (Blanket covers for guest beds are also nice but not necessary)
  extra pillows for guests

Colored and patterned sheets are pretty, but, except for those to be used in the master bedroom, white may be more practical. Solid white or those with simple colored, scalloped borders can be used with any color scheme, whereas the more elaborate ones may be restricted to use in one room. Monogrammed sheets are, of course, lovely and luxurious.

Bath Linen (for one-bathroom apartment)

4 large bath towels
4 matching hand towels
4 washcloths
4 guest towels, linen or terry cloth
2 bath mats
1 shower curtain

The quantity need not be doubled for an additional bathroom, since towels can be interchanged or used in various color combinations.

Table Linen

If you have a formal dining room:

1 damask, linen, or lace tablecloth, large enough to fit a table that can seat eight people (at least 72 by 108 inches)
8 matching dinner napkins
2 or 3 52-inch-square tablecloths to fit card tables for additional seats at dinner parties or for bridge
1 or 2 sets of linen place mats (for 8) with matching napkins
12 linen or cotton (preferably permanent press) napkins in several colors to go with odd plastic mats, etc.
2 sets (4 or 6) of hard-surface plastic mats for every day
1 set (6 or 8) of more elaborate hard-surface mats for informal entertaining
Large paper dinner napkins
24 cocktail napkins, paper or cloth

You may not feel that you will have any need for a damask cloth in the foreseeable future, but remember that it is ideal for a buffet table as well as a sit-down dinner. When you use a cloth with a pad under it, every inch of space on the table is useful, which is not true when hot plates must be placed on individual mats or trivets. Also, a tablecloth inevitably adds a touch of elegance when you wish to depart from your usual informal way of entertaining.

Even though you may have no dining-room table for the present, damask will remain fresh and unspoiled for years. Accordingly, while you may not feel you can afford to buy your future formal table covering yourself, it makes an ideal gift from a relative or godparent.

Marking Linen

Katherine Leigh Adams, who will marry Brian Charles Jamison may have the linen initialed with her married initials, KJ or KJA or her future husband's last initial, J. Often the single initial embellished with a scroll or pretty design is more effective than three initials, and the cost may be less. The bride who chooses to keep her own name may have her last initial and that of her husband divided by a dot or design: A·J

Towels are marked at the center of one end, so that the monogram shows when they are folded lengthwise in thirds and hung over a rack.

Long rectangular tablecloths are marked at the center of each long side, midway between table edge and center of cloth.

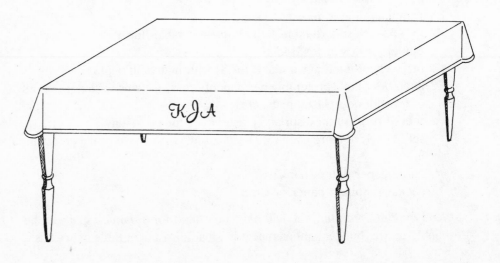

Small square cloths are marked in one corner midway between center and corner, so that the monogram shows on the table.

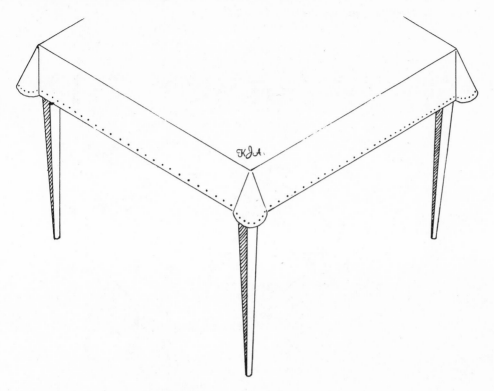

Dinner napkins are marked diagonally in one corner or centered on a rectangular fold.

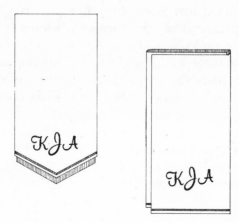

Sheets are monogrammed so that when the top is folded down, the letters can be read by a person standing at the foot of the bed. Pillowcases are marked approximately two inches above the hem.

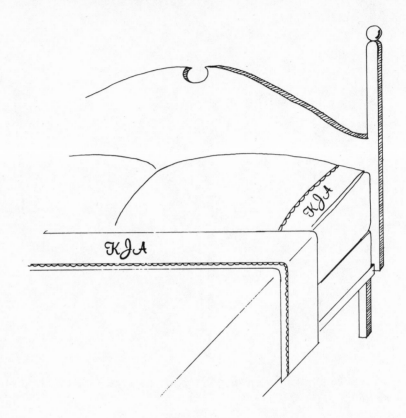

As soon as wedding invitations are received, the recipients start to think about what they should send as a gift. Therefore, before the invitations are sent out, Kate and Brian should place their names on the bridal registers of the gift shops and department stores in their city and choose the patterns and articles that appeal to them most. (See page 196 for the type of information usually requested on bridal registry forms.) They can also select the monogram style they prefer, and the stores will register this information for their customers' use. Friends and relatives may use this bridal registry service to help them select a gift they know will be appreciated. Kate and Brian should try to choose items from various price ranges so that all who come to the store and consult the bridal registry can find something that will fit their pocketbooks as well as their preferences.

China

Today the stores are filled with colorful sets of pottery, plastic ware, and china in every variety imaginable. The problem is not to find sufficiently attractive tableware but to decide among the many to choose from. There is, however, one important thing for a couple to keep in mind. That is the matter of replacements. They should remember that in the case of a pattern not easily replaced, breakage will leave them handicapped. Therefore it is always wise to ask if a pattern is in open stock, meaning that the pattern is usually stocked by the store and pieces are available singly. Another useful hint is that soap-bubble-thin glass, or glass that is very finely chased or cut, naturally goes best with delicate porcelains, whereas the heavier glassware is best suited to pottery and plastics.

The one requirement for a table set entirely with china is that it be in harmony, meaning that it have some matching detail such as texture or perhaps a repeated note of color. In other words, service plates of one variety, bread-and-butter plates of another variety, centerpiece of another, dishes for sweets of another, and candlesticks of still another would look like an odd-lot table selected at random unless all those pieces match in the ways suggested.

The following lists are what the couple should *basically* have to start out with. If their funds are limited and if they are not given enough dinner and dessert plates, for instance, to complete eight or twelve place settings, they may add a piece or two as often as they can, completing one place setting at a time rather than buying two or three more dinner plates and still having an incomplete setting.

Everyday Dishes

The bride will need a complete set of 4 or 6 settings of inexpensive china, pottery, stoneware, or unbreakable plastic ware, which also comes in most attractive patterns. This set should include:

dinner plates
dessert plates (used also for salad)
cereal dishes (used also for soup, puddings, fruit)
cups or mugs
saucers if cups are chosen
cream pitcher and sugar bowl

Dishes for Entertaining

The bride may prefer to be given complete place settings. A typical place setting includes:

dinner plate
salad plate (may double as a dessert plate)
bread and butter plate
cup
saucer

Optional:

soup cup (two-handled, for both clear and cream soups)
cream pitcher and sugar bowl
platters and vegetable dishes
demitasse cups
gravy boat
sauce bowl

Or she may prefer to receive sets of 8 or 12 dinner plates, dessert plates, butter plates, etc., in different patterns, as long as they are compatible.

If the bride prefers variety to a uniform set of china, she must choose her accompanying items carefully. Glass, silver, pewter, wood, and easy-to-care-for stainless steel may be combined with any china to make a charming dinner table. To go with the varied dinner and dessert plates, she will need:

8 or 12 glass or silver butter plates
8 or 12 glass salad plates (the crescent-shaped ones are pretty and take up less space on the table)
12 cups and saucers in any pattern
8 or 12 demitasse cups and saucers in any pattern
2 platters and 3 vegetables dishes of silver or stainless steel
1 cream pitcher and sugar bowl of silver, glass, or stainless steel

Other useful items (which may be of any material or style that the bride prefers) are:

4 salts and peppers (silver, glass, stainless steel, wood, china, or a combination of silver and wood)
1 salad bowl and servers (wood or glass)
1 bread dish (silver or wicker)
1 gravy or sauce boat (silver or china)
condiment dishes (glass, china, or pottery)

1 water pitcher (any material)

1 teapot

1 silver coffeepot or a presentable coffee maker (such as stainless steel or glass, whether electric or not) that may be brought from the kitchen for serving after-dinner coffee

8 or 12 small bowls for serving ice cream with sauce or a "runny" dessert (glass dishes look very pretty on a plate with a colorful pattern showing through)

3 or 4 pots and casseroles, in which food is cooked and served in the same dish

1 electric warming tray (an invaluable aid when entertaining without help)

4 trays (wood, metal, or plastic)

Glasses

Glasses are so easily broken, and good glasses so expensive to replace, that a bride who wishes to have a matching set for any length of time should have far more than she actually needs to start out with.

In order to save her expensive glass for parties, she should have for everyday use and for casual entertaining:

6 tumblers

8 or 12 old-fashioned or "on-the-rocks" glasses

8 or 12 wineglasses

8 or 12 iced tea or highball glasses

6 or 8 Pilsners or beer mugs

Beyond this, she should have, depending on the number of place settings she has decided upon:

goblets

liqueur glasses

stemmed sherbet glasses

champagne flutes

Silver

Many brides request that they be given pewter or stainless steel platters, serving dishes, or similar items rather than silver, as they require little care and are more durable. However, although Kate may ask for stainless steel eating utensils for daily use, nothing can replace a set of beautiful sterling flat silver on the dinner-party table. Often the parents of the bride or the groom choose the flat silver as their gift to the couple. There are innumerable patterns; the bride whose home is "traditional" may choose one of the older, more ornate patterns, and she who leans toward "modern" will probably prefer a very plain design. Each has its advantages. The modern, undecorated piece is easier to clean, but it also shows wear and tear more quickly and is sometimes marred by scratches. Whichever Kate and Beth choose they should remember that it is probably the silver they will use all their lives, and possibly their children after them, so it is safer to select a pattern that is not extreme in any way—neither too severely modern nor so ornate that it easily appears outdated.

As with china, it is wise to complete one place setting at a time rather than have twelve forks and no knives. If they are getting their china and silver place setting by place setting, Kate and Beth will simply start out with smaller parties. This is not a disadvantage, however. A young woman who has had little practice in party-giving will do far better to begin with two or four guests and enlarge the number as her experience increases.

The necessary silver for one place setting is:

1 large fork

1 small fork

1 large knife

1 dessert spoon (can double as soup spoon)

1 teaspoon

1 butter knife

In addition, assuming that the bride hopes eventually to have complete service for twelve, the following items are necessary. They need not be in the same pattern as the above list:

12 soup spoons

3 serving spoons (tablespoons in the chosen pattern may be used)

2 serving forks

12 after-dinner coffee spoons

2 gravy or sauce ladles

4 extra teaspoons (for sugar, condiments, etc.)

Optional, and often received as wedding presents:

oyster forks
salad or fish forks (broad tines)
sugar tongs
butter server
ornamented spoons for jellies or jams
cake knife
pie server
steak knives

If the flat silver is monogrammed, a triangle of block letters, lastname initial below and the first-name initials of bride and groom above, goes well on a modern pattern. When Katherine Leigh Adams marries Brian Charles Jamison

K B
J

If a single initial is used, it is the last-name initial of the groom.

If the bride or groom has inherited silver, or silver marked with maiden initials or family initials, and the couple wants to add to it, the same initials should be used.

Any initialing should be simple and legible in style. Elongated Roman goes well on modern silver, and Old English on the more ornamental styles.

Monograms on flat silver have always been placed so that the top of the letter is toward the end of the handle. In other words, when the piece is on the table, the monogram is upside down as seen by the diner at that place. People have asked me why it should not be inscribed so that the letters are legible to the user, rather than to someone across the table who probably could not see it in any case. This seems quite reasonable and, despite the fact it is not the customary way, I see no reason why, if you prefer, you should not have your silver marked in that position.

A wedding gift of silver may be marked if the giver is absolutely sure that it is something the bride truly wants and that no duplicate will arrive, but generally it is safer to leave it unmarked so that it can be exchanged if desired.

3

EXPENSES AND BUDGETS

Whatever size or style of wedding you choose, it is the careful, thoughtful planning and the atmosphere—not the cost—that makes it beautiful. It is not how much you spend but how you spend that matters. While a large, elaborate wedding may cost thousands of dollars, there are many ways in which you can save without stinting. Very often the simplest wedding is the most tasteful. The following list is intended only to explain the traditional division of expenses. Many of these items may be omitted entirely without making your wedding any the less beautiful and meaningful.

There are many variations not only in ways to save, but also in how the costs are divided. Today the bride and groom often pay their own wedding costs, particularly when the wedding is a second one for either or both. The groom's family often offers to pay a share and it is quite acceptable for the bride's parents to accept this offer, especially if the groom and his family would like a larger or more elaborate reception than the bride's parents can afford. Use these pages as a guide, and make your own adjustments.

The Traditional Division of Expenses

Expenses of the Bride and Her Family

Services of a bridal consultant and/or a secretary
Invitations, announcements, and enclosures

The bride's wedding dress and accessories

Floral decorations for ceremony and reception, bridesmaids' flowers, bride's bouquet (in some areas given by groom)

Formal wedding photographs and candid pictures

Videotape recording of wedding

Music for church and reception

Transportation of bridal party to ceremony, and from ceremony to reception, if hired cars are used

All expenses of reception

Bride's presents to her attendants

Bride's present to groom, if she wishes to give him one

The groom's wedding ring, if it is to be a double-ring ceremony

Rental of awning for ceremony entrance and carpet for aisle, if desired and if not provided by church

Fee for services performed by sexton

A traffic officer, if necessary

Transportation and lodging expenses for pastor or rabbi if from another town and if invited to officiate by bride's family

Accommodations for bride's attendants, if required

Bridesmaids' luncheon, if one is given by the bride

Expenses of the Groom and His Family

Bride's engagement and wedding rings

Groom's present to his bride, if he wishes to give her one

Gifts for the groom's attendants

Accommodations for groom's attendants, if required

Boutonnieres for the groom's attendants

Ties and gloves for the groom's attendants, if not part of their clothing rental package

The bride's bouquet in areas where local custom requires it

The bride's going-away corsage

Corsages for immediate members of both families (unless bride has included them in her florist's order)

The minister's or rabbi's fee or donation

Transportation and lodging expenses for the minister or rabbi if from another town and if invited to officiate by the groom's family

The marriage license

Transportation for the groom and best man to the ceremony

Expenses of the honeymoon

All costs of the rehearsal dinner, if one is held

Bachelor dinner, if he wishes to give one
Transportation and lodging expenses for groom's parents

Bridesmaids'/Honor Attendant's Expenses

Purchase of apparel and all accessories
Transportation to and from the city or town where the wedding takes place
A contribution to a gift from all the bridesmaids to the bride
An individual gift to the couple
A shower and/or luncheon for the bride

Ushers'/Best Man's Expenses

Rental of wedding attire
Transportation to and from location of wedding
A contribution to a gift from all the groom's attendants to the groom
An individual gift to the couple
A bachelor dinner, if given by the groom's attendants

Out-of-Town Guests' Expenses

Guests who come from a distance pay their own transportation and lodging expenses. The parents of the bride or groom should assist their relatives and friends by making reservations or sending them hotel and motel information, and may offer to pay any expenses they wish to assume, but are not at all required to do so. They may also accept the offers of local friends and relatives to provide accommodations for out-of-town guests in their homes.

Exceptions to Tradition

As mentioned before, there are many acceptable exceptions to these guidelines. They might be completely reversed in the case of a young girl who is an orphan or who comes from another country. In those circumstances, the groom's family could well arrange and pay for the entire wedding.

In some areas, and among certain ethnic groups, the groom traditionally provides the liquor or champagne for the reception. In others, the groom is expected to buy all the flowers for the wedding party. On occasion, because the bride is wealthy and the bridesmaids are not, she may pay for their wedding costumes or their transportation costs. But these are local customs or special situations, and for the majority of people the division of expenses listed above is considered essentially correct.

There is, however, one gradual but noteworthy change occurring. Perhaps because of the increased cost of giving a wedding, or perhaps simply because the groom and his family take a more active part in the planning and preparations than they used to, they are more and more often sharing some, or all, of the expenses with the bride's parents. In some cases the groom simply wants to include more friends and relatives than the bride's family can afford, and rather than leave out people close to him, he (or his parents) offer to help, sometimes by paying for the liquor, other times by renting a hall or whatever seems best. This is no longer considered "insulting" to the bride and her family, and in many cases it has resulted in closer ties between the families. The offer should, however, come from the groom and his parents; the bride's family should not ask for assistance. If their budget is limited, they should simply restrict the wedding arrangements to what they can afford.

When the groom's family assumes a fair share of the costs, they become co-hosts with the bride's parents. Therefore, the wedding invitations should go out in their name too.

Planning a Budget

A carefully prepared budget, based upon what you and your parents can afford, will spare you the nightmare of impractical plans that must be constantly changed—or unnecessary debts. Whether you are planning an elaborate wedding with 300 guests or a simple ceremony with 30 friends present in your own home, a realistic budget will help you make your preparations more smoothly and happily.

A budget for a large wedding should include your allotments for each of the expenses listed on the next page. The budget for a simple wedding should include the items that you cannot provide yourself and intend to purchase, and also the way in which you will take care of other requirements. For example:

Photographs—Uncle John will take them for us as his wedding gift.

Wedding cake—Aunt Doris baking it as her gift.

With imagination and good planning, a beautiful wedding can be held within any limits. Whatever you plan, keep to your budget, or the worry and insecurity will get your marriage off to a bad start.

Costs for large formal weddings can range from tens of thousands of dollars to just a few thousand dollars, depending on the number of guests, the elaborateness of the wedding, and local costs and customs. This table shows the items that must be budgeted for. Amounts are not included since they change so rapidly. When making up your budget, put down what you think you can allow and adjust the figures as you get estimates from the professionals involved.

The best way to plan is to begin with your fixed costs, such as the minister's or rabbi's and organist's fees, gifts for your attendants, postage, wedding rings, etc. Subtract that total from your available funds and see what amount you have to work with. This will give you a guide as to how much you have left for variable costs, such as limousines, a photographer, and the rehearsal dinner and reception.

Budget Categories

Bride's gown
Bride's accessories
Invitations/enclosures
Announcements
Postage
Flowers for ceremony
Flowers for reception
Bride's bouquet
Flowers for bride's attendants
Corsages
Boutonnieres
Organist's fee
Cantor/vocalist/instrumentalist fee
Music for reception
Sexton's/facility fee
Minister's or rabbi's fee
Limousines for bridal party
Photographer
Videographer
Bride's gifts for attendants
Groom's gifts for attendants
Bride's ring
Groom's ring
Marriage license
Accommodations for bride's attendants
Accommodations for groom's attendants
Rehearsal dinner (per person cost)
Bridesmaids' luncheon
Bachelor's dinner
Reception expenses (per person cost)
Wedding cake

4

PLANNING THE WEDDING

Careful, detailed planning is the most essential element in arranging the perfect wedding. If your wedding is to be a small and simple affair, you and your family will be able to attend to most of the details yourself. If you are dreaming of a large, elaborate wedding, you will do well to use professional help. Without it, you and your parents, as well as your groom, could arrive at the ceremony harassed, exhausted, and with no energy left to enjoy your own wedding day.

Remember that although final decisions are traditionally up to you and your family if they are assuming most of the costs, your bridegroom has a place in the wedding, too. As the beginning to your life together, consult him, and when appropriate, his family, on all major questions from beginning to end. This does not mean you must ask your groom's parents' advice every step of the way; rather that you help make them feel involved when you share details and your excitement with them as plans progress. Asking their advice on such things as the seating of their friends and relatives is not only courteous but their suggestions will be of great assistance to you as well.

Your mother, as hostess, has every right to take part and assist you in your decisions. It is your wedding, however—not hers—and where there is a difference of opinion, the final choice should be yours. There is nothing sadder than a bride and her mother at swords' points over plans for a wedding, an event which should be one of the happiest in their lives and which they should thoroughly enjoy together. The problems usually arise when a mother has for years dreamed of a lavish wedding for her daughter and the daughter and her fiancé want a very simple ceremony. Occasionally a young woman wants a more expensive wedding than her family can afford, but it is more often the other way around.

The two areas of argument are generally the guest list and the formality of the reception. When your parents are paying for the wedding, they naturally feel that their special friends should be included. You may not feel any affection for these people and wish instead to have more of your own friends and those of your groom. In general, your mother should accede to your wishes, but you must compromise somewhat too. Often your parents' friends care far more about you than you realize, and surely you in turn care for some of them. Keeping those two facts in mind, even at a small wedding, your parents have the right to invite those of their friends who are closest to you and your family, drawing the line sharply if you wish, so that other, more distant acquaintances will not be hurt.

The formality of the wedding relates directly to the size. If you and your parents have agreed on a large wedding, your mother may make it as elaborate as she wishes. If she feels she can afford an orchestra, a sit-down meal, and so on, you should be happy to go along.

However, again, if you and your fiancé wish to keep your wedding small and your reception simple, the decision should be yours, and one that your mother respects.

Your mother may well have more experience than you in planning menus, decorations, and so on. Therefore, you will be wise to abide by her advice in those areas. But when it comes to the personal matters—choosing your attendants, your dress, and the clothes of the attendants, making honeymoon plans—the final word is yours. Listen to your parents' advice; they may have some very good and practical thoughts; but after listening and making a careful choice, insist politely, but firmly, on having your wedding as you wish it.

The plans discussed in this chapter include every aspect of the most elaborate wedding possible. Many of you will neither wish nor be able to carry out all of them; but the etiquette is the same regardless of the size of your wedding, and it is up to you to choose those elements which best fit into your plans.

Unlike Kate and Brian, who are planning a very elaborate wedding, David and Susan are planning a very small, simple morning ceremony, followed by a brunch. Ben and Beth, like many couples today, are paying the cost of their own wedding, with little or no financial assistance from their parents. Beth is wearing her mother's wedding gown, friends are providing the reception meal, and Ben and Beth are making their own tapes of favorite classical music to be played during the reception. They are serving only champagne, punch and soft drinks with no open bar. These are areas of savings which enable them to invite the number of guests they wish to have share their special day that by no means diminish the charm and loveliness of their wedding. Although they are paying the costs of their wedding, they have chosen to issue the invitations in Beth's parents' name, which is as acceptable as sending them in their own names would be.

The First Decisions

As soon as the engagement is announced, you and your fiancé decide approximately when you want to be married. Three to six months is an ideal period between engagement and marriage. Your first step is to go to your minister or rabbi and find out on which days, and at what hours, your church or synagogue is available. After setting a tentative date, you and your mother start to make the arrangements for the reception. You may decide that you would like to use the facilities of your parents' club, which will also provide the catering. If they do not belong to a club, you will find that hotels and restaurants are happy to render the same services. If the reception is to be held at your parents' home, your mother may hire a caterer who will provide all catering needs and equipment. In Kate's and Brian's case, the church is large and the clubrooms spacious, so they estimate they will be able to invite approximately 250 guests. They must make this decision as soon as possible so that the manager will be able to plan on whatever equipment will be necessary, and so that invitations can be ordered at once.

Having found her family's club available on the date agreeable to her minister, Kate Adams confirms the day and time. Local custom dictates the most popular hour for weddings. In the South, weddings are often held in the evening since the days are so warm. Catholic weddings that include a nuptial mass were traditionally held at noon or earlier to accommodate those who fast before Mass. This is no longer necessary, but many Catholic weddings are still held at that hour. Four or five o'clock in the afternoon is the usual hour for a formal Protestant wedding in the East. Less formal ceremonies may be held at almost any hour, often depending on the travel plans of the bride or groom. It is best, if possible, to plan the reception immediately following the wedding, so that out-of-town guests—and sometimes the bridal party—are not left wondering what to do and where to go. In any event, there is no fixed rule. The hour of the wedding is decided by these customs and the wishes of the couple themselves. Kate and Brian decide that they would like to be married at 4:30 P.M.

The Guest Lists

Four lists are combined to make up the master list—those of the bride's parents, the groom's parents, the bride, and the groom. It is up to the bride's mother to discuss with the groom's mother (by phone or letter) the number of invitations available to her. If both families live in the same community, the invitations should be evenly divided. Since some names would surely be duplicated, the bride's mother should let the groom's mother know how many extra spaces are available to her. But since Kate lives in Connecticut and Brian comes from Minnesota, Mrs. Adams tells Mrs. Jamison that only fifty of their relatives and friends will be able to attend. Therefore, although invitations may be sent to many more out-of-towners, Mrs. Jamison knows that she may safely add extra names, if she wishes, to her list. Both families may invite a few more than the total allowed them, since there will always be some refusals other than those expected.

It is most important that the two mothers make up their lists *realistically*. The groom's mother must make every effort to stay within the number of places allotted to her, since the limit set by the bride's family is often dictated by necessity. If she feels she simply *must* invite more than the number specified, she and her husband should offer to pay a share of the expenses sufficient to cover the additional costs. The other alternative is for her to plan a reception for the bride and groom after the honeymoon, to which the friends who could not be included at the wedding are invited.

Many people prefer not to send invitations to those acquaintances who cannot possibly attend. They feel it might appear that they are merely inviting those friends to send a gift. Such friends should receive an announcement, or possibly an invitation to the church only, neither of which carries any obligation whatsoever.

When the church is large, the bride's family and the groom's may invite all their personal acquaintances and also their business associates to the church ceremony. Their lists for the reception should be restricted to more intimate friends. Were the wedding in the house or chapel, and the reception limited to relatives and very close friends, announcements would be sent to all those who could not be included at all. Both bride and groom should check carefully with parents and grandparents to be sure that no old family friends are overlooked.

Ceremony and reception invitations should also be sent to the following people:

The person who performs the ceremony, and his or her spouse, if any.

The fiancés(ées) of invited guests (When the bride knows the name of the fiancé(e), she sends him or her a separate invitation. If she does not know it, she should try to get the name and address from the one she knows. Should this be very difficult, she may enclose a note with the latter's invitation, saying, "Dear Pamela, we would be delighted if you would bring your fiancé.")

The parents of the bridesmaids (not necessary, but a nice gesture whenever feasible)

The bridal attendants (who enjoy them as mementos of the occasion) and their spouses

The groom's parents—for the same reason (they are not expected to reply, since their attendance is taken for granted, unless they have called or written a personal note to explain their absence)

Small children, even though they cannot be included at the reception (they are usually thrilled with an invitation to the church ceremony)

People in mourning, even though they may not attend

One member of a married couple should never be invited without the other. Also, both members of an unmarried couple living together should be invited.

The Problem of Children

One of the greatest and most common problems is that of restricting the number of children attending the reception. In large families with dozens of cousins, nieces, and nephews, the costs may swell astronomically if they are all invited. And yet some relatives feel so strongly that their children should be included that they threaten to refuse the invitation if the children are left out.

There is no easy answer. It would be most unfriendly and in the poorest of taste to write "No children" on the invitations. There are two things you can do to discourage the youngsters' attendance. You may enclose a note to those who are most understanding, explaining that costs and space prevent your asking all children under a certain age. You may also talk to close friends and relatives, explaining the problem and asking them to help by spreading the word.

Having done this, you must make no exceptions. Outside of your own children or your own brothers and sisters, you must refrain from inviting one child under your age limit, or the hurt feelings incurred will far outweigh the money saved.

The Formality of the Wedding

There are three categories of weddings—formal, semiformal, and informal. The formality necessarily is related to the location of the ceremony and reception, the size of the wedding party, and the number of guests. While a wedding in a church or synagogue may range from most formal to least formal, a ceremony held in a house always lends itself more to informality—unless the house is a mansion. There are infinite variations, but the table on pages 00–00 demonstrates the main differences among the three categories.

Many of the items are interchangeable and must be adapted to fit each individual situation. However, the list should give you some assistance in knowing what you are talking about when you tell your clergyperson or your caterer that you want a "formal," a "semiformal," or an "informal" wedding.

	Formal	*Semiformal*	*Informal*
Bride's dress	Long white gown, train, veil optional	Long white gown, veil optional	White or pastel cocktail dress or suit or afternoon dress (sometimes, very simple long gown)
Bridesmaids' dresses	Long or according to current style	Long or according to current style	Same type of dress as worn by bride
Dress of groom and his attendants	Cutaway or tailcoat (see chapter 6)	Sack coat or tuxedo (see chapter 6)	Dark business suit or jacket (see chapter 6)
Bride's attendants	Maid or matron of honor, 4–10 bridesmaids, flower girl, ring bearer (optional)	Maid or matron of honor, 2–6 bridesmaids, flower girl, ring bearer (optional)	Maid or matron of honor, 1 or 2 children (optional)
Groom's attendants	Best man; 1 usher for every 50 guests, or same number as bridesmaids	Best man; 1 usher for every 50 guests, or same number as bridesmaids	Best man; 1 usher if necessary to seat guests
Location of ceremony	Church, synagogue, or large home or garden	Church, synagogue, chapel, hotel, club, home, garden	Chapel, rectory, justice of the peace, home, garden
Location of reception	Club, hotel, garden, or large home	Club, restaurant, hotel, garden, home	Church parlor, home, restaurant
Number of guests	200 or more	75 to 200	75 or under
Provider of service at reception	Caterer at home, or club or hotel facilities	Caterer at home, or club or hotel facilities	Caterer, friends and relatives, or restaurant
Food	Sit-down or semi-buffet (tables provided for bridal party, parents, and guests); hot meal served; wedding cake	Buffet (bridal party and parents may have tables); cocktail buffet food, sandwiches, cold cuts, snacks, wedding cake	Stand-up buffet or 1 table for all guests; may be a meal or snacks and wedding cake

	Formal	Semiformal	Informal
Beverages	Champagne; whiskey and soft drinks (optional)	Champagne or punch for toasts; whiskey and soft drinks (optional)	Champagne or punch for toasts; tea, coffee, or soft drinks in addition
Invitations and announcements	Engraved	Engraved	Handwritten or telephoned invitations; engraved announcements
Decorations and accessories	Elaborate flowers for church, canopy to church, aisle carpet, pew ribbons, limousines for bridal party, groom's cake (given to guests in boxes), engraved matchbooks or napkins as mementos, rose petals or confetti	Flowers for church, aisle carpet, pew ribbons, rose petals (other items optional)	Flowers for altar, rose petals
Music	Organ at church (choir or soloist optional); orchestra for dancing at reception	Organ at church (choir or soloist optional); strolling musician, small orchestra, or records for reception; dancing optional	Organ at church; records at reception optional

Bridal Consultants and Secretaries

Anyone who plans a very large and formal wedding would be wise to consider engaging the services of a bridal consultant or secretary. Such help is inestimable, when hundreds of guests are expected, in relieving the bride's family of routine, time-consuming chores. The advice of the consultant and the details—lists, addresses, bills—that are taken care of by the secretary ensure that the bride and her mother will arrive at the wedding far less exhausted than would otherwise be possible.

Ordering the Invitations

Invitations should be ordered as soon as the date is set and the lists prepared. During busy seasons they may take weeks to arrive, and time must be allowed for addressing and stuffing the envelopes. Once the invitations are decided upon, ask the printer if you may have the envelopes in advance. They can be addressed in advance, which saves a tremendous amount of time later, when the bride is usually busier with other arrangements.

Kate and Brian or Kate and her mother go to the stationer's, choose the style, texture, and type from the examples provided, and order the required number.

Correct wording and a detailed description of invitations and announcements will be found in Chapter 5.

David and Susan are having a small wedding and have decided to hand write their invitations, so their purchase is lovely note paper available from a stationery store.

Choosing the Attendants

The average formal or semiformal wedding party includes four to six bridesmaids and at least that many ushers. There may be more ushers than bridesmaids, as the number is often determined by the "one usher for fifty guests" rule, but there should not be more bridesmaids than ushers. The attendants are invited to serve soon after the engagement is announced. Since they are invariably relatives or close friends, the invitation is issued in person, by telephone, or if they live far away, by letter. If it is feasible, Kate and Brian should invite those friends in whose weddings they have served to take part in their own. Unless it is absolutely impossible, no one should refuse the honor when asked to be an attendant.

When one of the bridesmaids or ushers is forced to withdraw unexpectedly, you may, even up to the last day or two, ask another close friend to fill in. Friends should not be offended by a late invitation, but rather should be flattered that you feel close enough to count on them in an emergency.

Kate and Brian discuss the size and formality of the ceremony, carefully considering whom they would like for attendants and which of their friends will most probably be able to come. Kate decides to have a maid of honor, four bridesmaids, a flower girl, and a ring bearer. Brian will have a best man, four ushers, and two junior ushers.

David and Susan, who are not having a large wedding, will have two of their own children serve as their attendants. David's son will be his father's best man, and Susan's daughter will be her mother's matron of honor.

Ben and Beth are having a more elaborate wedding than David and Susan, but a much smaller wedding than Kate and Brian. After discussing their wishes with Ben's ex-wife to have his children included, Beth has asked Ben's daughter to be her flower girl and Ben has asked his son to be a junior usher.

The Bride's Attendants and Their Duties

Maid or Matron of Honor

The bride's closest sister is almost always chosen for this position. Kate's younger sister, Lisa, will be maid of honor. If Kate had no sister near her age, a cousin or best friend would serve. If Brian's sister were a close friend of Kate's, she would be a logical choice. A married woman, or matron, may be chosen instead of a maid of honor, and on rare occasions there are both a maid and a matron of honor. In this case the "maid" takes precedence, holding the bouquet and serving as a witness. It is up to the bride and groom to decide whether or not they wish to have an extra usher to escort the matron of honor out of the church. Later her husband will join her at the bridal table, or as her escort.

Lisa's most important duty is to be aide and consultant to Kate, relieving her of as many chores as she can, especially on the wedding day. During the ceremony she holds the bride's bouquet, helps adjust her veil, and arranges the train when Kate turns to leave at the end of the service. She stands next to the couple in the receiving line, sits on Brian's left at the bridal table, and helps Kate change into her going-away costume. Although a groom's father may serve as best man, a bride's mother should not act as matron of honor. Her duties as a hostess are most important, and quite distinct from those of matron of honor. It is not obligatory, but a maid of honor who is not a member of the bride's family usually arranges for, or gives a shower for the bride.

Bridesmaids

Formerly bridesmaids were literally unmarried "maids"; now they may be either single or married contemporaries of the bride. If the groom has a sister, she is usually included, as are close relatives of the bride. It is better not to choose as a bridesmaid a girl who is noticeably pregnant unless she and the bride are totally comfortable about it. Bridesmaids have few special duties other than forming the bridal procession and, if the bride desires, standing with her in the receiving line. Later they circulate among the guests, acting as deputy hostesses.

Any or all of them may give showers, or they may join in giving one large shower, and they often give a luncheon for the bride or attend one given by her. Generally they give her a joint present, engraved with their names or initials, as well as personal wedding gifts.

Bridesmaids are responsible for paying for their costumes and seeing that they are properly fitted. The considerate bride will think of her bridesmaids' pocketbooks when she chooses their dresses. They also pay all transportation expenses, but the bride is responsible for their lodging from the time they arrive until the day after the wedding.

Junior Bridesmaids

Junior bridesmaids are girls usually between eight and fourteen who are too big to be flower girls and too small to be bridesmaids. Their duty is merely to walk in the procession. They do not give showers or stand in the receiving line (unless asked), and whether they are included at the rehearsal dinner and showers depends on their ages.

Flower Girl

The flower girl is often a young relative of the bride, between three and seven years old. Kate's flower girl is the daughter of a close friend, who is one of the bridesmaids. She walks directly before the ring bearer in the procession, and directly behind him when they leave the altar. She does not go to the rehearsal dinner, although she must be a part of the rehearsal, nor does she stand in the receiving line. The flower girl's dress and accessories are paid for by her family. It may be similar to the bridesmaids' dresses, or it may be in a child's style but in a matching color or it may be, at the bride's choice, a white dress.

In the case of Kate's wedding, her flower girl's mother is also a member of the wedding party and therefore available to watch over her. For Beth, however, her new stepdaughter, Christy, is serving as her flower girl and is unchaperoned since her own mother won't be present. Kate should ask one of her bridesmaids to keep an eye on Christy, check her appearance, make sure she is present for formal pictures, that she can manage her meal, is escorted to the ladies room, etc. at those times when Kate and Brian are busy with their guests and with other responsibilities.

Ring Bearer

A small boy between three and seven is chosen for this duty. Kate chooses her four year old brother. The most appropriate dress is short pants with an Eton jacket, preferably white but occasionally navy. Small editions of the ushers' costumes are not in good taste.

The ring bearer carries the ring, or a facsimile, on a white velvet or satin cushion. If the ring is actually the one that is to be used, it should be fastened to the cushion with a very thin thread or placed over a firmly fixed hatpin. The best man takes it from the cushion at the proper moment. The ring bearer immediately precedes the bride in the procession.

If you are having a double-ring ceremony, it is safer to have the actual rings to be used carried by the best man and the maid of honor because of the possibility of the ring bearer confusing them, and the complications of where the child should stand to deliver each one.

Train Bearers and Pages

Train bearers and pages may be included in the wedding party, but the presence of too many children can be distracting and can detract from the bride or from the solemnity of the ceremony. When children are included in a wedding party, their parents, if not also members of the wedding party, should be invited guests so that they may assume responsibility for their children after their duties are completed.

The Groom's Attendants

Best Man

Often a brother or cousin serves as best man, but if the groom has neither, it may be a friend, or frequently his father. Brian's best man is Thomas Coleman, who was his roommate at college.

Next to the bride and groom themselves, the best man is the most important member of the wedding. His duties are numerous and most important. They vary with the circumstances, depending on the nature of the plans for the wedding and the amount of time he has free to place at the groom's disposal before the ceremony. The important thing is that he relieve the groom of as many details and as much responsibility as possible.

Some time before the wedding, with the ushers' approval, he selects the gift that they will present to the groom. He makes the purchase, arranges for monogramming or marking if necessary, and collects the money from each usher. He also makes the presentation to the groom, usually at the rehearsal dinner.

Tom helps Brian pack for his honeymoon and sees that the clothes Brian will change into after the wedding are packed in a separate bag and taken to where the reception will be held.

He must see that Brian is dressed in plenty of time. He must also be sure to get the wedding ring and the clergyperson's fee from Brian and put them in his own pocket. He hands over the ring promptly at the correct moment in the service. If there is to be a ring bearer, the best man is responsible for the ring until it is safely placed on the cushion. He must be prepared for any emergency.

Toward the end of the reception, when Kate and Brian leave to change to their traveling clothes, he helps Brian dress, takes care of his wedding clothing, and finally sees that he has with him everything necessary for the wedding trip. Money or traveler's checks, passports, car keys, baggage-check stubs, plane, train, or boat tickets—these are all too easy for the groom to overlook in his excitement.

Tom may deliver the luggage of both bride and groom to the airport, pier, or station from which they will leave, seeing that it is properly checked and giving the claim checks to the groom. If he is especially thoughtful, he may even arrange to have flowers or a bottle of chilled champagne delivered to their hotel room just before their arrival.

He is in charge of whatever transportation the couple will use to leave the reception, and he keeps these plans secret and the car hidden to foil any practical jokers. He sees that their luggage is in the car, and he himself drives them to its hiding place or else arranges to have the car delivered at the moment of their departure.

The best man is responsible for delivering the minister's or rabbi's fee on behalf of the groom. He may do this before the ceremony while they are waiting to enter the church, or if he is not driving the bride and groom to the reception, he may return to the vestry immediately after the recessional to deliver the envelope. When the fee is given in the form of a check, it is made out to the minister rather than to the church, unless the minister requests otherwise.

Tom enters the chancel from the vestry immediately after Brian and stands behind the groom and slightly to his left, in such a position that he can conveniently give the wedding ring to him when the minister calls for it.

At the end of the service, if the best man is not to walk out with the maid of honor, he leaves through a side door while the procession goes down the aisle. If it is cold, he quickly goes around to the front of the church to give the groom his hat and coat. Sometimes the sexton does this for him, but in either case the best man always hurries to see the bride and groom into their car. In the absence of a chauffeur, the best man drives them to the reception. If he is to walk out with the maid of honor, he performs the same duties immediately after walking down the aisle.

After seeing that there is nothing to be done for Brian while he is in the receiving line, Tom may mingle with the guests until the bridal party sits down at the bridal table. He sits on the bride's right, and it is his responsibility to make the first toast to the bride and groom and to read any telegrams or messages that have arrived. He keeps the telegrams carefully and delivers them to Kate's parents, so that they may be acknowledged when the couple returns from their honeymoon. He is also the first man to dance with Kate after her groom, her father-in-law, and her father have had their turns.

When the couple is ready to leave, the best man escorts the groom's family to the dressing room for their farewells. He then leads the couple through the waiting guests to the door. When they have pulled away in a shower of rose petals, he may then breath a sigh of relief and join the rest of the wedding party in a final celebration.

Ushers

The groom selects as ushers his brothers, relatives of his own age, and closest friends. If the bride has brothers of the same age, they are usually included. One who is particularly reliable or experienced may be chosen as head usher. He is responsible for seeing that the others arrive at the rehearsal and church on time, assigning them to certain aisles, and designating the ones who will escort the immediate family. The head usher himself may escort one or both of the couple's mothers, unless there are brothers of the bride or groom in the party, who would naturally escort their own mothers.

There should be one usher to every fifty guests, and their responsibility is to see that all guests and family members are seated, insofar as possible, where they wish to be. Two ushers are appointed to put the pew ribbons in position, and two others to lay the carpet. (For a more detailed description of these activities, see Chapter 8.) When those duties are completed, and the two mothers seated, all the ushers go to the back of the church to walk in the procession. At the reception they are seated at the bridal table, if there is one, but they do not stand in the receiving line.

They pay for their own wedding clothes—whether bought or rented—with the exception of their gloves, ties, and boutonnieres, which are given to them by the groom if not included in the rental package.

The ushers attend the bachelor dinner, if there is one, or occasionally arrange it themselves. They also contribute to a joint gift to the groom, selected by the best man.

Junior Ushers

Junior ushers are usually young relatives of the groom—between ten and fourteen. They are dressed like the ushers, and their only duty is to walk in the procession. If there are two, they are frequently chosen to place the pew ribbons.

Lodging for Attendants and Guests

Some time before the wedding Kate and Brian must think about lodging for the attendants and family friends who will come from out of town. Ideally the attendants are put up with relatives and friends, but this is not always possible. If they must be lodged in hotels or motels, the costs are paid by the bride for her bridesmaids and by the groom for his ushers. The transportation expenses to and from the location of the wedding, however, are paid for by the attendants.

Guests, whether relatives or friends, pay for their own lodging unless either family offers to assume that expense. But Kate or her mother should reserve accommodations well ahead of time to ensure comfortable rooms. They may send folders and price lists to the people involved and let them select their own place, or they may simply choose what they consider the nicest spot and advise the guests about the reservations and the prices.

If the groom's family lives in another city, it is up to his mother to notify the bride or her mother how many will be coming and what accommodations they will need.

Planning the Ceremony

The details of the wedding ceremony are planned in conjunction with your pastor or rabbi. If you wish to write your own vows or to include a special passage or poem in the service, this must be planned and approved in advance. Most faiths require that parts of the service read a certain way; others allow couples greater freedom in writing their own services. Your pastor's or rabbi's directions must be followed in this. If you would like a choir or a soloist to sing special selections or an instrumentalist to play during the service you must arrange this with the sexton, the organist, or the church or synagogue wedding coordinator. You would discuss the selections with the organist. Detailed suggestions for wedding music will be found in Chapter 13.

As soon as you and your fiancé have decided on a tentative date or an approximate time for the wedding, you should call your church or synagogue office. If you are away at college or living in another area, you should write. This must be done promptly, since all other plans will depend on the result of this conversation. During this first call, if possible, you should arrange an initial appointment with the minister or rabbi to which you and your fiancé go together. If he is out of town, you should go yourself to discuss dates, hours, and details.

Most pastors and rabbis will want to have a series of additional appointments with you and your groom before the ceremony. These counseling sessions give him or her and the two of you the opportunity to discuss your feelings about marriage, commitment, children, your faith, and other areas of your relationship. If you are being married in your own church or synagogue, these visits will be easy and informal. But if you are not affiliated with a church or a synagogue or are, perhaps, being married in your groom's church, you must make a little more effort. Be sure that you know the minister's name and correct title. If he or she does not know you, certain papers may be required—birth or baptismal certificates, divorce decree, or others. When you call or write for your first appointment, ask just what will be needed.

If your fiancé is not of the same faith as you are but plans to be converted, your minister or rabbi will give him religious instruction. If he does not plan to join your faith, your minister or rabbi will still wish to discuss important aspects of the faith with him, and time should be set aside for this.

Other matters to discuss with your pastor or rabbi are:

- Length of ceremony
- Number of guests church or synagogue will comfortably hold
- Whether, when, and how photographs and/or a video recording may be taken before, during and/or after the service
- If a second minister or rabbi will be participating, how arrangements should be made
- When to make an appointment with the organist to select music
- What kind of floral arrangements/decorations are permitted
- How to arrange access for the florist; the disposition of flowers after the ceremony
- Whether there is a room for dressing prior to the service, if you require one
- If you should arrange for the services of a traffic officer
- Whether rice, rose petals, bird seed, etc. are permitted to be thrown outside the building
- If you want an aisle carpet, whether one is provided

- Whether the synagogue provides a canopy
- Whether there are restrictions on your dress or your bridesmaids' ensembles (sleeves, neckline, length, and so on)
- What fees are required for the use of the facility; the organist; for additional musicians; for the sexton; for the minister or rabbi

Be sure to make a reservation for the rehearsal at the time you make the reservation for your wedding ceremony.

If any restrictions do exist, you must of course respect that decision.

Frequently the groom or his family belongs to a different congregation, and they may be very close to their own minister or rabbi. There is no reason why he or she cannot assist at, or even perform, your service, as long as your minister or rabbi agrees. This is also true when a relative or close friend of the bride or groom is a member of the clergy. If you decide to be married by someone from another church or synagogue, you and your fiancé should meet with him or her in addition to your own minister or rabbi, if possible. If one is from far away, the arrangements must be made by letter or telephone, but the visiting clergy may wish to make a preliminary visit to meet the minister of the home church or synagogue and become familiar with its arrangement and customs.

Whoever performs the service, the pastor or rabbi of the church or synagogue where the marriage takes place receives a fee. Visiting clergy may or may not accept a fee depending on their relationship with the couple, in which case a gift would be appropriate and in any case, travel and lodging expenses are paid by for the family which invited the visiting clergyman to officiate.

Planning the Reception

In planning your reception, you must weigh the advantages of having it at home against those of holding it elsewhere. A club, hotel or catering hall are the usual choices for a wedding outside the home, but some unusual places sometimes serve as sites of weddings. If novelty appeals to you, check into facilities that are available in your area. For example, historic buildings can be rented for weddings, as can ferry boats and gardens in parks. Of course, the time of year and the size of the wedding are important considerations.

There is no question but that it is easier to hold the reception outside your home. You and your mother still have to make the plans and the decisions, but most of the actual work will be done for you. A reception at home, however, has a certain warmth and intimacy that cannot be duplicated in a hall or even a private club.

To hold a reception in your home, or the home of a friend or relative, no matter what the size of the reception, entails a good deal of work. A very small party can of course be handled entirely by you, with the help of your mother and some friends. By preparing food in advance and freezing it, by keeping the menu and the decorations as simple as possible, the home wedding can be both inexpensive and, within reason, easy to manage. But to have more than twenty or thirty guests with any degree of pleasure and relaxation for you, you must have professional help. For a reception of more than thirty guests, this means a caterer. Depending on your requirements and the size of his or her firm, a caterer will provide food, the wedding cake, the serving staff, crystal and china, tables and chairs, and some will provide tents, dance floors, and innumerable other services.

The best way to find a reliable caterer is to ask people who have used their services. You may, of course, look in the yellow pages and at advertisements in local magazines and newspapers, but if you do, check references and if possible, sample their food and see their equipment.

If you use a caterer, either for a wedding at home or at another site, be absolutely sure that every service to be provided and the *total* itemized costs are given to you in a contract. As with any contract, read it carefully and make sure you understand and agree to all terms and costs before you sign.

Specifically, be sure the following points are covered:

- Detailed menu and how it will be served
- Beverages—open bar, champagne, soft drinks
- Wedding cake
- Number of serving staff
- Whether gratuities are included
- Number and set up of tables and chairs
- Delivery charges
- Deadline for guest count
- Overtime charges
- Coat check facilities
- Tents or marquees
- Whether glass and china are insured against breakage
- Whether taxes are included in estimate

A Reception at a Club, Hotel, or Catering Hall

Hotels, restaurants, private clubs and catering halls generally offer wedding "packages" depending on the time and elaborateness of your reception. When selecting a reception site outside of your home or other than a site requiring an outside caterer, such as an historic building or garden, make a list of initial questions to ask the restaurant or club manager:

- Is a wedding package offered?
- If so, what does it include and what does it cost?
- Are substitutions permissible?
- What food and drinks will be served at the cocktail hour? During the reception? Will brand name liquors be served? If not, how much more would the cost be to serve them? Will there be an open bar for the cocktail hour? For the entire reception?
- What does a sample place setting consist of?
- May you sample food and observe a party arranged in the room which may be selected for your reception?
- Will the establishment provide printed directions to the site for you to include with your invitations?
- Is insurance against china and crystal breakage included in the costs stated? If not, is it required and at what cost?
- What are your choices of table linen colors?
- May you see a book of wedding cakes they provide and sample the type you want? May you provide your own wedding cake (baked by a friend or at a bakery)?
- Is there a florist the restaurant or club manager uses and recommends and if so, does he or she have a book you may look at to select arrangements? If you prefer to provide your own decorations, how can this be arranged?
- May the reception be extended an extra hour? At what time do servers go on overtime pay? What would the overtime charges be?
- Are all gratuities included in the stated costs?
- Is there a special rate for providing food and beverages for the musicians and photographers?
- Is there a room available for formal portraits to be taken if they aren't taken at the ceremony site? Is there an additional charge for use of this room?
- What are the parking arrangements for guests?

Be sure to have all these details spelled out before signing a contract. Also, be sure to make note of dates with which you should communicate specific details to the club or restaurant manager—such as the final guest count, arrangements for an outside florist or baker to deliver flowers or wedding cake, whether you plan to have a groom's cake, and so on. You should also see how tables will be set up; if you want a bridal table, how many guests the other tables seat comfortably; where speakers will be located if music will be amplified; whether you require a table for placecards or gifts; and where a receiving line may be placed.

The Wedding Cake

No matter what type of reception you plan, one of the essential ingredients is your wedding cake. It may be ordered through a caterer, who delivers it shortly before the hour of the reception; from the restaurant or club; or it may be ordered from a bakery, in which case arrangements may be needed to have someone deliver it to the reception. If the wedding is very small, there is no reason why a member of the family or a close friend who is a skillful baker should not make your wedding cake.

A white cake with elaborate icing, the bride's cake is sometimes placed as a centerpiece on the bridal table, if there is one, but more often sits on its own table at a vantage point from which it may be admired by everyone. Or it may also form the centerpiece for a buffet table.

The icing is usually all white, although it may be entirely or partly of color, perhaps to match the gowns of the bridesmaids. Pastel flowers in soft pink or yellow are lovely, because these are delicate, romantic colors. The cake may be in the shape of a heart or molded into a "wedding ring," but the prettiest and most impressive, I believe, is the round two- or three-tiered cake, often surrounded or topped by fresh flowers or greens. Bells or a replica of a wedding ring may top the cake in place of flowers. They are in better taste than the little bride and groom dolls sometimes used. Kate chooses a three-tiered cake with just a touch of soft pink in the frosting flowers to blend with her bridesmaids' dresses.

You may also have a second cake called a "groom's cake." Almost always a dark fruitcake, this is a disappearing item, owing largely to the expense. For years this cake was baked in advance, cut up into small squares, and packaged in pretty little white boxes bearing the bride and groom's initials in silver. The cost of the labor involved in doing this today, and the increased price of the initialed boxes, makes it prohibitive to many people. But it is a delightful custom, and the cake, which each guest takes home, makes a lovely memento of the wedding.

Because it is such a charming idea, close friends or relatives of the bride or groom sometimes offer to bake and wrap a groom's cake as a wedding gift. In this case they should not go to the expense of ordering boxes but may wrap the cake in shiny white paper tied with white satin ribbon.

Another type of groom's cake is a chocolate cake as opposed to the bride's white cake. It is placed on a separate table from the one from which the refreshments are served. People who prefer chocolate go to that table for their serving, incidentally helping to lessen the crowd around the bride's table.

Ordering the Flowers

The services of a florist should be requested as soon as the wedding date is determined. The florist should be told what will be required—flowers for the wedding party, boutonnieres, corsages, flowers for the ceremony site and possibly the reception. Specific details, such as colors and style, should be confirmed as soon as you know the style and colors for your gown, those of your bridal party, your mothers' and grandmothers' dresses, container sizes for the ceremony site, and table linen colors during the reception, if the florist is providing decorations and centerpieces.

In most parts of the country all flowers, including her own bouquet, are part of the bride's responsibility. She sometimes provides corsages for the two mothers and grandmothers, but in most cases the groom orders these and the one that the bride will wear when they go away.

In certain geographic areas it is customary for the groom to buy the bride's bouquet. When this is true, the corsage may form the center of the bouquet or arrangement, and it is removed before she throws the bouquet to her bridesmaids.

The groom provides the boutonnieres for the best man, the ushers, his and the bride's fathers, and himself.

To simplify ordering and floral deliveries, both the bride's and the groom's orders may be placed with the same florist. If the bride and groom are paying the costs of their own wedding, as are Beth and Ben, it makes no difference since the entire order will be paid on one bill. If the couple's wedding costs are being paid according to the traditional division of expenses by their parents as they are for Kate's and Brian's wedding, then the florist can be instructed as to how to divide the bill.

One of the key considerations when determining your flower order is the season of the year. However much you love lillies of the valley, they are practically impossible to buy except in the spring. Don't set your heart on one variety; let your florist help you choose a flower that will be appropriate not only to your wedding, but to the season, as well.

Deciding your flower order should be a pleasurable experience and one into which you put your creativity and careful thought. Your choice of flowers and their sweet, fresh appearance and fragrance symbolize new beginnings. (For more detailed descriptions of flowers and arrangements, see Chapter 13.)

Photographs

The photographer's time must be reserved as soon as possible, especially for candid pictures of the wedding and reception. The formal portraits should be taken when the wedding dress is ready. Kate has hers done at the final fitting. This is important if you intend to give that picture to the newspapers with your wedding announcement, which should be sent in at least three weeks ahead of your wedding date. It is for this reason that the groom does not usually appear in the picture accompanying the announcement—he does not get his wedding clothes until the day of the wedding, and therefore his picture cannot be taken far enough ahead.

A small print of your formal picture in a silver frame, with or without initials and date, makes an ideal present for your bridesmaids. Otherwise it is not necessary to give your attendants copies, although they may order them if they wish.

The candid pictures cover much of the wedding day, certainly from the time the bride finishes dressing until the end of the reception. You will find the pictures of the reception far more satisfactory if you ask one of your friends or relatives to tell the photographer which guests you would especially like pictures of from a list you have made ahead of time. Otherwise you may end up with snaps of people whom the photographer considers attractive but who are of little interest to you.

Do not permit the photographer to take pictures during the wedding ceremony or to follow the bridal party up the aisle. Provided your clergyman agrees, the photographer may remain at the back of the church, taking pictures of you entering and leaving, but I know nothing more distracting or less dignified than the sound of the shutter and the flash of a strobe while the service is in progress.

You may be fortunate enough to have a friend who enjoys—and is good at—taking pictures. If your friend Mary offers to take your wedding pictures as a favor, you should do your best to pay her for the cost of her film and printing. If she suggests that she do it as a wedding gift, be thankful and accept with pleasure!

Formal pictures of Kate's and Brian's bridal party are taken as soon as the members arrive at the reception. Occasionally they are taken before the couple leaves the church for the reception, if the churchyard or garden makes a particularly lovely setting. Pictures are taken of the bride and groom alone, the couple with the bridesmaids, and the couple with the entire wedding party. These are followed by photographs of the newlyweds with each set of parents and, if they wish, with other members of the immediate families. Divorced parents should not appear in the same photograph. Each one should have a picture taken with the couple separately. Stepparents are included if they are on friendly terms with the bride and groom. This picture taking often causes considerable delay in starting the receiving line and the festivities, and many people ask why it must be done then. The answer is that it is the only practical time. It is virtually impossible to fit picture taking in before the ceremony, and if Kate and Brian wait until they are about to leave the reception, the costumes and hairdos of the bridal party cannot possibly look as fresh as when they first arrive. The formal picture-taking will also go much faster if all people who are to be photographed remain nearby. But Mrs. Adams should instruct the photographer to start immediately and finish the procedure as soon as possible.

Many photographers make up thank-you cards which contain a small photograph of the bride and groom. These are charming mementos of the wedding, as long as the bride adds her own personal note of thanks to the printed message. The most satisfactory variety is a card with slots to hold the picture. The blank cards may be given to the bride as soon as she wishes so that she may keep up with her thank-you notes. Then, as soon as the pictures are printed, she slips them into the slots and mails the already written notes. Remember, however, before ordering these cards, that they cannot be mailed until the pictures are received, sometimes several weeks after the wedding. Charming as they are, this can be upsetting to those who send presents and embarrassing to the bride whose thank you notes are then sent very late.

When selecting a photographer, you should ask to see samples of his or her work to be sure it is of the quality and mood that you want. There are also several questions that you should ask before signing a contract:

- Is a wedding package offered? If so, what does it consist of? For example, Kate and Brian would want an album for themselves, one for Kate's parents, and one for Brian's mother. David and Susan might not want an album at all but rather extra copies of candid photos to send to friends and to keep in their own album. They would want to know if an alternative to a package would be available.
- What does it cost for additions to a package?
- What is the timing and what are the costs for formal portraits of the bride for newspaper announcements?
- What is the number of pictures to be taken at the wedding and the reception, and before the wedding, if desired?
- May the proofs be purchased?
- What is the number of photographs in the standard album?
- What is the size and cost of extra albums?
- Will the photographer stay through the entire reception or just through the cutting of the cake?

Videotaping

The videotaping of your ceremony must be cleared with your minister or rabbi before you arrange to have it done. There usually are specific guidelines which should be discussed with the videographer, such as his or her placement during the ceremony, whether certain portions of the ceremony will have to be re-staged if taping is not allowed during the actual ceremony, etc.

Contact several video studios and make appointments to see videotapes of weddings they have taped. Look carefully not only at the actual quality of the tape, but also at how it has been edited. Is the editing smooth or are there jumps, dark portions, and gaps? Is the sound clear? Does it cover the things you would want covered at your ceremony and reception? Ask key questions before signing a contract, and make comparisons, since the prices vary widely.

- Does the video studio offer a wedding package? If so, of what does it consist?
- What do additional copies cost?
- Are their additional costs for a video portrait of the wedding party and other groupings?
- Are there separate costs for taping the ceremony and the reception?
- How long will the videographer stay through the reception?

Ben and Beth have a good friend who is a professional videographer. She has offered to tape their wedding as a gift to them, including a section on Beth and her attendants getting ready and leaving for the ceremony. Even though this is a gift, it is perfectly all right for Beth and Ben to tell her of particular shots they would like her to take and to make suggestions of what is important to them, as long as they don't make excessive demands.

Music

If, as Kate and Brian do, you intend to have an orchestra for dancing at your reception, it should be hired immediately after setting the wedding date. Many popular orchestras are literally booked over a year in advance.

The size and formality of the wedding determine the type of music at the reception. If the reception is held under a large tent cover or in a ballroom or huge reception area, there can be a full orchestra, or even two so that there will be continuous music. Sometimes the orchestra leader will have a string section for soft background music before the dancing begins, as well as the dance band.

At smaller weddings, a strolling guitarist, a pianist, a trio, or even tapes piped in through a house tape system provide appropriate background music. Even with these, a small space can be cleared for dancing, if you wish.

The orchestra leader or musician will ask you and your groom what selections you would like, and you should be prepared with a list of your favorite pieces. (For the order of dancing at the reception, please see Chapter 9.)

The necessity for discussing the selection of music for the ceremony with the sexton and organist has already been mentioned. For specific suggestions, consult Chapter 13.

Planning Your Honeymoon

In addition to planning the important items already discussed, there are many, many other details to be taken care of. During your engagement period, you and your fiancé will enjoy making your honeymoon plans. Ideally, you will both want the same type of honeymoon, but if one of you wants to go camping and the other prefers life in a resort hotel, you must compromise. Spend a few days in a tent, and another few at a resort. Whatever you do, compromise. Don't start your married life by making a stubborn stand. You can always plan another vacation later to please the desires of the one who has compromised this time.

Feel free to consult your parents and friends and especially other newly-weds. They may have excellent suggestions about places they visited and enjoyed which might otherwise never occur to you. Also, talk to a travel agent. It is their business, and they can give you all the information you will need.

Philosophically, your honeymoon should be a private time shared only by the two of you, immediately following your wedding. Sometimes, however, there are circumstances which necessitate a variation. David, for example, has an important business meeting in Florida the week following his and Susan's wedding. They have decided that Susan will accompany him to the meeting location, after which the two of them will go on to the Bahamas for their "official" honeymoon, putting the stress of business and wedding behind them.

Ben and Beth are concerned that Ben's children be included in part of their time directly following the wedding. They have arranged to rent a small cottage on the coast for three days after their wedding, taking the children and Ben's sister with them. His sister will then take the children back home to their mother while Ben and Beth go on to Hawaii for two weeks. This arrangement helps create a feeling of family with the children, but also allows Ben and Beth time alone as they begin their life together.

Whether you travel to another location or simply stay at home for your honeymoon, it should be a time free of work, outside pressures, well-meaning friends who would like to entertain you, and even other family members. There will be plenty of time to share your happiness in one another with them after your honeymoon.

Bride's Check List

The best organized weddings are the ones where every detail has been thought of in advance. Thinking of those details is only the first step, however. Keeping a master check list, whether this one or one you write yourself, ensures that nothing is left to chance.

Your timetable should start three to six months before your wedding, and your master check list should be kept in a convenient place where you can consult it regularly, checking off items as they are attended to and adding even more details that may be special to your plans.

Three to Six Months in Advance of Your Wedding:

☐ Decide on the type of wedding and reception you want

☐ Consult your clergyperson to select the date and hour of your wedding

☐ Determine the location of your reception and reserve the club, hotel, restaurant or hall if it is not to be at home

☐ Engage a caterer if your reception is to be at home

☐ Determine the number of guests you are able to invite

☐ Choose attendants and ask them to serve

☐ Order invitations and announcements

☐ If you wish, order notepaper for thank-you notes, some monogrammed with your current initials and some monogrammed with your married initials for later on

Three Months in Advance of Your Wedding:

- [ ] With your fiancé, make appointments for counseling with your minister or rabbi and for discussing music, decorations and procedures during the ceremony with the minister or rabbi, sexton and organist
- [ ] Order your gown and those of your attendants
- [ ] Make out your guest list and ask the groom and his family to send you theirs. Tell them approximately how many guests they may invite
- [ ] Make an appointment with a photographer for your formal portraits and reserve his or her time for the day and time of your ceremony and reception
- [ ] If you plan to have live music at your reception, hire the band or the musician, or a disk jockey if you plan to have taped music for dancing
- [ ] If your wedding will be at home, make arrangements now for repairs, painting, cleaning, etc.
- [ ] Begin shopping for your personal and household trousseaus
- [ ] Select china, crystal and silver patterns
- [ ] Select gifts for your bridesmaids and a gift for your groom if you intend to give him one

Two Months in Advance of Your Wedding:

- [ ] Hire limousines, if necessary, for transporting the bridal party to the ceremony and from the ceremony to the reception
- [ ] Notify your attendants about their fittings and accessories. If possible, have shoes dyed in one lot
- [ ] List your selections at local gift and department store bridal registries, with your groom if possible. Tell your mother and your maid of honor where you are registered so that they can tell guests who ask them
- [ ] At the time of, or soon after the final fitting of your wedding dress, have formal bridal photographs taken
- [ ] Make detailed arrangements with the manager of your reception site or caterer including menu, table arrangements, decorations, linens, parking, and so on
- [ ] Make medical and dental appointments, and a hairdresser appointment if you intend to have your hair done on the day of your wedding
- [ ] Address and stuff wedding invitations
- [ ] Make housing arrangements for out-of-town attendants and obtain hotel and motel information for guests from out of town

- [ ] With your groom, select wedding rings
- [ ] Mail invitations four to six weeks in advance of your wedding
- [ ] Remind your groom or the best man to arrange fittings and reserve any rented formalwear for himself and the groomsmen

One Month in Advance of Your Wedding

- [ ] Check with your groom about his blood test and the marriage license
- [ ] If you are displaying wedding gifts, begin setting up tables for them
- [ ] Record all gifts and write thank-you's as they arrive
- [ ] Make a list of your honeymoon clothing and be sure it is cleaned, pressed and ready to pack
- [ ] Check on all accessories for you and your attendants
- [ ] Make final arrangements with all professionals who are working with you— florist, photographer, reception manager or caterer
- [ ] If you are changing your name, do so on all documents such as driver's license, credit cards and bank accounts, etc. Both you and the groom should obtain and complete change of address forms at the local Post Office
- [ ] Check your luggage to be sure it is adequate and in good condition
- [ ] Check on the advisability of a floater insurance policy to cover your wedding gifts—especially if you are displaying them
- [ ] Arrange the details for a bridesmaids' luncheon if you wish to give one
- [ ] Address your announcements, stamp them, and give them to your mother or a friend to mail the day after your wedding
- [ ] Make the arrangements for a place for your bridesmaids to dress
- [ ] Plan the seating for the bridal table and parents' table(s) at your reception and make out place cards for them
- [ ] Send your wedding announcement to the newspapers with your wedding portrait if you wish
- [ ] Notify your wedding party of the time of the rehearsal

Two Weeks in Advance of Your Wedding:

- [ ] Confirm hotel, motel or other lodging arrangements for your bridal party
- [ ] Confirm flower order and deliveries with florist

One Week in Advance of Your Wedding:

☐ Pick up gifts for your attendants

☐ Give final count of guests to reception manager or caterer

☐ Reserve afternoon to have friends and family visit to view your gifts, if on display

☐ Plan quiet dinner for just you and your fiancé

☐ Plan light refreshments for your attendants if they will be changing at your house

The Morning of the Wedding:

☐ Have hair done, or shampoo and arrange it yourself

☐ Make sure any orders not being delivered are picked up (flowers, food, etc.)

☐ Eat breakfast—no matter how nervous you may be

Two Hours Before the Ceremony:

☐ Have your attendants arrive at your house to prepare to dress and to assist you with any last minute details

☐ Meet your attendants at the hotel, if you will be changing there instead, or one hour before at a reserved room at the place your ceremony will be held

One Hour Before the Ceremony:

☐ Apply make-up and dress, making sure to cover face before dressing so as not to get make-up on your gown

☐ Ushers should arrive at place of ceremony at least 45 minutes before to plan duties and to seat any early arrivals

One Half Hour Before the Ceremony:

☐ Groom and best man arrive at place of ceremony

☐ Background music starts

☐ First guests arrive and are seated

☐ If you have dressed at home, you and your attendants go to church or synagogue and wait in private room

☐ Best man checks last-minute arrangements with minister or rabbi and gives him or her the fee

Fifteen Minutes Before the Ceremony:

☐ Family members and honored guests (godparents, for example) arrive and are seated "within the ribbon" or in the pews near the front

Five Minutes Before the Ceremony:

☐ The groom's mother and father arrive and she is escorted to her seat, followed by her husband

☐ The bride's mother is escorted to her seat in the front row

☐ The white carpet, or aisle runner, is rolled down the aisle

☐ The bride's father takes his place with his daughter

☐ The attendants take their places in the proper order for the processional

☐ At precisely the time stated on the invitation, the music starts and the ushers lead the procession down the aisle

5

INVITATIONS AND ANNOUNCEMENTS

The wording of formal traditional engraved wedding invitations and announcements is as fixed as the letters of the alphabet. The third-person form has been used for countless years, and the replies are written in exactly the same style. The invitation is usually sent in the name of the bride's parents, since they pay most of the expenses and are the "hosts," but if the groom's parents are assuming a full share of the costs, the invitations should be in their name also.

Invitations to a formal wedding are mailed four to six weeks beforehand; those to a small wedding may be sent as late as ten days before the ceremony.

The Style of the Invitations

Your stationer will show you several grades and shades of paper from which you make your selection. Ivory, soft cream, and white are all correct. If you can afford it, you will do well to choose the heaviest-weight paper. It may cost a bit more, but its fine appearance and feel make it worth the extra expense. Whether the paper is flat or has a raised plate mark or margin is up to you. Either the large double sheet, which is folded a second time to go into the envelope, or the smaller double sheet, which goes in unfolded, is correct. The tissues inserted by the engraver used to be necessary to avoid blotting or smudging but improved printing and engraving techniques have made them obsolete, and you may discard them if you wish.

The stationer will show you a number of typeface also. Shaded Roman, antique Roman, and script are very popular. Simple styles are in better taste than ornate and flowery engraving. If the bride's father's family has a coat of arms, she may properly have it, or a crest only, engraved without color at the top center of the invitation. If you cannot afford engraved invitations, less expensive thermographed ones are equally acceptable.

Stuffing the Envelopes

One of the unique conventions about wedding invitations is that there were always two envelopes. The invitation (folded edge first) and all enclosures were put in the inner envelope, facing the back flap. This envelope was then placed unsealed in the outer envelope, with the flap away from the person inserting it. Both envelopes were always addressed by hand.

While it is still perfectly correct to order both envelopes, it is also correct to omit the inner one. In the interests of economy and conservation, and because today we prefer the simplest and most practical customs, the inner envelope now seems superfluous.

The Inner Envelope

If you choose to have an inner envelope, it bears only the names of the people to whom the mailing envelope is addressed. A married couple's inner envelope is addressed to "Mr. and Mrs. Anderson" with neither the first names nor address. When an invitation is sent to several young children, the inner envelope is addressed to "Judith, Stuart and Shaun." If the outer envelope is addressed to the parents and a young daughter, her name is written on the inner envelope below her parents' name: "Miss Ann Kennedy." Intimate relatives may be addressed on the inner envelope as "Aunt Kate and Uncle Fred" or "Grandmother."

The Outer Envelope

Wedding invitations are always addressed to both members of a married couple, even though the bride may know only one, or knows that only one will attend. Invitations to an unmarried couple are addressed to Mr. John Burns and Ms. Mary French.

No abbreviations are used in addressing wedding invitations. A person's middle name may or may not be used, but if it is, it must be written out in full. "Street," "Avenue," and the name of the state may not be abbreviated.

Children over thirteen should, if possible, receive separate invitations. Young brothers and sisters may be sent a joint invitation to "The Misses" or "The Messrs. Jones." If there are both boys and girls, the address may read:

The Messrs. Jones
The Misses Jones

"Miss Mary Jones" or "The Misses Jones" may be written below "Mr. and Mrs. Franklin Jones," but "The Messrs. Jones" should receive a separate invitation.

Although it is generally not considered in the best of taste to address an envelope to "Mr. and Mrs. Franklin Jones and Family," there are circumstances when relationships are so complicated or children so numerous that this seems to be the only solution. It should be done only, however, when every person living under the same roof is intended to be included in the invitation.

When a bride and groom feel that they can accommodate a few extra people, they may address envelopes to their single friends: "Miss Sheryl Smith and guest" or "Mr. Robert Black and guest." If you are using inner envelopes, this should go only on the inner one, but if you are not, it may appear on the outer envelope, or you may indicate that a guest is welcome by a personal note included with the invitation: "Dear Sheryl, we would be delighted to have you bring a date if you would like to."

Return Addresses

Regardless of the many years during which it has been considered bad taste to put return addresses on wedding invitations, it is time to change the rule. There are two excellent reasons. First, the U.S. Postal Service requests that all first-class mail bear a return address. Second, it provides an address to which invited guests may send replies and gifts, especially when no R.S.V.P. appears on the invitation.

Some addresses are embossed on the back flap of the envelope without inking. They often go unnoticed, however, and the envelope is discarded before the receiver realizes that no other address appears. Therefore I see no reason why you should not order the return address to be engraved legibly on every mailing envelope.

Conventional Wording and Spelling

Some of the specific rules regarding formal wedding invitations are as follows:

1. The invitation to the wedding ceremony in church reads: "Mr. and Mrs. Howard William Adams request the honour"—traditionally spelled with a "u"—"of your presence . . ."

2. The invitation to the reception reads: "Mr. and Mrs. Howard William Adams request the pleasure of your company . . ."

3. Invitations to a Roman Catholic wedding may replace the phrase "at the marriage of" with "at the marriage in Christ of . . ." They may also add, beneath the groom's name, "and your participation in the offering of the Nuptial Mass."

4. No punctuation is used except after abbreviations, such as "Mr. or Mrs." or when phrases requiring separation occur in the same line, as in the date.

5. Numbers in the date are spelled out, but long numbers in the street address may be written in numerals.

6. Half-hours are written as "half after four," never "half past four."

7. Although "Mr." is abbreviated, and Junior may be, the title "Doctor" is more properly written in full.

8. If the invitation includes the handwritten name of the recipient, the *full* name must be written out. The use of an initial—"Mr. and Mrs. Robert S. Roth"—is not correct.

9. The invitation to the wedding ceremony alone does not include an R.s.v.p.

10. On the reception invitation, "R.S.V.P.," "R.s.v.p.," and "The favour of a reply is requested" are equally correct. If the address to which the reply is to be sent is different from that which appears in the invitation itself, you may use "Kindly send reply to," followed by the correct address.

Invitation to Church Ceremonies

The most formal wedding invitation, rarely seen today, has the name of the recipient written by hand:

Doctor and Mrs. John Huntington Smith
request the honour of

Mr. and Mrs. Brandon Williams

presence at the marriage of their daughter
Ellen Marie
to
Mr. Gary Alan Peters
Saturday, the first of November
at twelve o'clock
St. John's Church

The most common form, equally correct, is:

Mr. and Mrs. Howard William Adams
request the honour of your presence
at the marriage of their daughter
Katherine Leigh
to
Mr. Brian Charles Jamison
Saturday, the twelfth of June
at half after four o'clock
Village Lutheran Church
Briarcliff Manor

Wedding and Reception Invitation in One

When all the guests invited to the wedding are also to be invited to the reception, the invitation to both may be combined:

> Mr. and Mrs. Clay Francis Newberry
> request the honour of your presence
> at the marriage of their daughter
> Elizabeth Christine
> to
> Mr. Benjamin Steven Clark
> Friday, the second of October
> at half after five o'clock
> Church of the Redeemer
> San Francisco
> and afterward at the reception
> Bay Shore Country Club
> R.S.V.P.

Wedding Held at a Friend's House

Even though the wedding and reception are held in a friend's house, the invitations are written in the name of the bride's parents or sponsors:

> Mr. and Mrs. Eugene Braden Shanks, Jr.
> request the honour of your presence
> at the marriage of their daughter
> Ann Lea
> to
> Mr. John Jefferson O'Dell
> Saturday, the eighth of May
> at eight o'clock
> at the residence of Mr. and Mrs. Thomas Lockyer
> Evanston, Illinois
> R.s.v.p.

When the Bride's Mother is Divorced

On formal correspondence, a divorced woman formerly used her maiden name and her last name rather than her first name (Mrs. Stephenson Barnes). Although this is technically correct, most divorcées today use their first names rather than their maiden name, and few people would know who "Mrs. Stephenson Barnes" was.

Therefore it is now acceptable for a divorcée to send out her daughter's invitations as "Mrs. Virginia Barnes."

Mrs. Virginia Barnes
requests the honour of your presence
at the marriage of her daughter
(etc.)

When Divorced Parents Give the Wedding Together

In the event that relations between the bride's divorced parents are so friendly that they share the wedding expenses and act as co-hosts, both names must appear on the invitation. The bride's mother's name appears first:

Mr. and Mrs. Matthew Corwin Brown
and
Mr. and Mrs. Robert C. Shields, Jr.
request the honour of your presence
at the marriage of
Laura Jean Shields
(etc.)

If, however, the bride's parents are not sharing expenses, yet the bride wishes both parents' names to appear, a different situation exists. If the bride's mother is not contributing to the cost of the wedding the bride's father's name appears first on the invitation and he and his wife host the reception. The bride's mother is then only an honored guest at the reception.

When the Bride Has One Living Parent

When either the bride's mother or father is deceased, the invitation is issued only in the name of the living parent.

Mrs. [Mr.] John Whelan
requests the honour of your presence
at the marriage of her [his] daughter
Margaret Ann
(etc.)

However, there are circumstances when the bride very much wants to include the name of the deceased parent. This is acceptable, as long as the invitation does not appear to be issued by the deceased.

Together with their families
Deborah Ellen Keyes
daughter of Mary Ann Keyes and the late William Keyes
and
James Bryant Huseby
son of Mr. and Mrs. Silas James Huseby
request the honour of your presence
at their marriage
Tuesday, the twenty-first of November
(etc.)

When the Bride Has a Stepfather

When the bride's mother has been widowed or divorced and has recently remarried, the invitations are worded:

Mr. and Mrs. Raymond Jones Harper
request the honour of your presence
at the marriage of her daughter (or, Mrs. Harper's
daughter)
Kelly Elizabeth Quimby
to
(etc.)

If the bride's own father has no part in her life and her stepfather has brought her up, the invitation reads:

Mr. and Mrs. Raymond Jones Harper
request the honour of your presence
at the marriage of their daughter
Kelly Elizabeth Quimby
(etc.)

"Miss," "Ms." or "Mrs." is rarely used before the bride's name. The following two cases are exceptions:

When the bride has no relatives and her wedding is given by friends, the invitation reads:

Mr. and Mrs. Thomas Allen Harrell
request the honour of your presence
at the marriage of
their niece
Miss Rosemary Londen
to
Mr. Karl Andrew Rauch
(etc.)

A bride and groom who send out their own invitations would also use a title ("Miss," "Mrs."):

The honour of your presence
is requested
at the marriage of
Miss Dawn White
to
Mr. Michael Jordan
(etc.)

[or]

Miss Dawn White
and
Mr. Michael Jordan
request the honour of your presence
at their marriage
(etc.)

If the bride has brothers or sisters, or other relatives, the wedding may be given by them, and the invitations are sent in their names:

Mr. Timothy Hennessy
requests the honour of your presence
at the marriage of his sister
Stephanie Kristin
(etc.)

[or]

Mr. and Mrs. Steven Wise
request the honour of your presence
at the marriage of their niece
Susan Schiff
(etc.)

When the Bride is a Young Widow or Divorcée

Invitations to a young widow's second wedding may be sent by her parents exactly as were the invitations to her first marriage. The only difference is that her married name is used:

Doctor and Mrs. Barry Farnham
request the honour of your presence
at the marriage of their daughter
Carolyn Farnham Flood
(etc.)

A divorcée's second wedding ceremony may read the same way. The bride's name would be the one she is using, either her maiden name with her ex-husband's last name, or, if she has dropped her ex-husband's name, with her own middle and maiden name.

If the Bride is a More Mature Widow or Divorcée

A more mature woman whose parents are dead, or a divorcée who has been independent since her divorce, would generally send out her own invitations.

A widow's invitation would read:

The honour of your presence
is requested
at the marriage of
Mrs. George Saunders Simon
and
Mr. Craig Forsythe Douglas
(etc.)

A divorcée's invitation would read:

The honour of your presence
is requested
at the marriage of
Mrs. Ann Rogers Duker
(etc.)

If she prefers, she may drop the title and have her name read simply "Ann Rogers Duker."

Since David's and Susan's grown children are giving their wedding, the invitation may be issued in their names, with the bride's children listed before the groom's. When there are several children involved their names are given in age order, from oldest to youngest, in each family.

Mr. and Mrs. Andrew Romeo
Mr. and Mrs. Daniel Jordan
Mr. and Mrs. Frederick Ingram
request the honour of your presence
at the marriage of their parents
Susan Brown Jordan
and
David Andrew Ingram
Sunday, the Second of September
at three o'clock
at the St. James Club
Cos Cob, Connecticut

When the Bride Has a Professional Name

If the bride is well known by a professional name and has many professional friends to whom she wishes to send invitations or announcements, she may have her professional name in parentheses engraved below her real name on those invitations:

Pauline Marie
(Pat Bond)
to
Mr. Carl Louis Finelli

This is done by having "(Pat Bond)" added to the plate *after* the other invitations for those who know the bride only by her real name have been printed.

Military Titles

When the groom is a member of the Army, the Navy, the Coast Guard, the Air Force, or the Marine Corps, or is on active duty in the reserve forces, he uses his military title.

Officers whose rank is captain in the Army or lieutenant, senior grade or higher in the Navy have the title on the same line as their names:

Colonel Frank Burson
United States Army

Those with lower ranks have their name and title engraved in this form:

John McMahon
Ensign, United States Navy

In the case of reserve officers on active duty, the second line would read, "Army of the United States" or "United States Naval Reserve."

First and second lieutenants in the Army both use "Lieutenant" without the numeral.

A noncommissioned officer or enlisted man may have his rank and his branch of the service below his name or not, as he wishes.

Henry DeLucia
Corporal, Signal Corps, United States Army

[or]

Marc Josephson
Seaman Apprentice United States Naval Reserve

High-ranking officers of the regular armed forces continue to use their titles, followed by their branch of service, even after retirement, with "retired" following the service:

General George Harmon
United States Army, retired

When the father of the bride is a member of the armed forces, either on active duty, a high-ranking retired officer, or one who retired after many years of service, he uses his title in the regular way:

Colonel and Mrs. James Booth
request the honour of your presence
(etc.)

The name of the bride who is on active duty in the armed forces is written:

marriage of their daughter
Ann-Lee
Lieutenant, United States Army

Other Titles

Medical doctors, dentists, veterinarians, clergymen, judges, and all other men customarily called by their titles should have them included on their own wedding invitations, and on the invitations to their daughters' weddings.

Holders of academic degrees do not use the "Dr." unless they are always referred to in that way.

Women use their titles only when the invitations are issued by themselves and their grooms.

The honour of your presence
is requested
at the marriage of
Dr. Laurie Neu
and
Mr. Norbert Rudell
(etc.)

Otherwise, she is, "their daughter, Laurie."

The bride's mother preferably does not use the title "Dr." on her daughter's invitation. If she and her husband feel strongly that she should, the wording has to be, "Dr. Mary and Mr. Henry Smith request . . ."

The Double-Wedding Invitation

Double weddings almost always involve the marriage of two sisters, and the form is:

Mr. and Mrs. Henry Smart
request the honour of your presence
at the marriage of their daughters
Cynthia Helen
to
Mr. Steven Jones
and
Linda Caroline
to
Mr. Michael Scott Adams
Saturday, the tenth of November
at four o'clock
Trinity Church

The elder sister's name is given first.

In the rare event that two close friends decide to have a double wedding, the invitation reads:

Mr. and Mrs. Henry Smart
and
Mr. and Mrs. Arthur Lane
request the honour of your presence
at the marriage of their daughters
Cynthia Helen Smart
to
Mr. Steven Jones
and
Mary Alice Lane
to
Mr. John Gray
(etc.)

When the Bridegroom's Family Gives the Wedding

When the bride comes from another country, or from a great distance without her family, the groom's parents give the wedding and issue the invitations. This is also true if the bride's family disapprove of the wedding and refuse to take any part in it.

Mr. and Mrs. John Henry Pater
request the honour of your presence
at the marriage of
Miss Marie Dubois
to
their son
John Henry Pater, Junior
(etc.)

The announcements, however, should be sent by her own family, if possible, or by the groom's family including the name of the bride's parents.

Including the Groom's Family in the Invitation

The bride's family ordinarily arranges and pays for the wedding and reception. They are, therefore, the hosts, and the invitations are issued in their name.

However, there are occasions when the groom's family shares in, or pays the major part of, the wedding expenses. In such a case it seems only fair that their names appear on the invitations, since they are actually co-hosts. The wording would be:

Mr. and Mrs. Charles Goodman
and
Mr. and Mrs. George Gonzalez
request the pleasure of your company
at the wedding reception of
Julia Goodman
and
Roberto Gonzalez
(etc.)

A form followed in some foreign countries, and sometimes by foreigners living here, provides for a double invitation—the bride's on the left and the groom's on the right.

Mr. and Mrs. Bruno Cairo
request the honour of your
presence
at the marriage of their daughter
Maria
to
Mr. Francesco Conti
(etc.)

Mr. and Mrs. Robert Conti
request the honour of your
presence
at the marriage of their son
Francesco
to
Miss Maria Cairo
(etc.)

Alternatives to Traditional Invitations

Many people today find the traditional third-person wording too distant and formal for their tastes. This is not unreasonable, given our informal life-style, and it has led to the composing of some very beautiful personal invitations. The invitation may be engraved or thermographed just as formally as a traditional one, or, when the wedding is to be simple and untraditional, it may be printed on paper with a design or border, often in a color carrying out the color scheme of the wedding itself.

Here are samples of invitations that are in very good taste yet seem warmer than the traditional form.

My own particular favorite:

Our joy will be more complete
if you will share in the marriage of our daughter
Susan Hall
to
Mr. James Bogard
on Saturday, the fifth of June
at half after four o'clock
6 Sesame Lane
Oldtown, Massachusetts
We invite you to worship with us,
witness their vows and join us
for a reception following the ceremony
If you are unable to attend, we ask your
presence in thought and prayer.
Mr. and Mrs. Hugo Stone
(or, Anne and Hugo Stone)
R.S.V.P.

When the invitation is to come from both sets of parents, it might be worded:

Anna and David Solomon
Janice and Abraham Gold
would be honoured
to have you share in the joy
of the marriage of their children
Sharon
and
Elliot
This celebration of love will be held on
Sunday, the ninth of September
at five o'clock
Temple Shalom
Englewood, New Jersey
A reception will follow the ceremony
at the Palisades Lodge
Palisades Parkway
Kindly send reply to:
Mr. and Mrs. David Solomon
(address)

A bride and groom who want to write their own invitations yet would like a touch of formality might use the following form:

Beth Holland and Christopher Saladino
invite you to attend
their marriage
on
Saturday, October the twenty-first
at three-thirty
The Hopewell School
Richmond, Virginia
A reception on the grounds will follow the ceremony
R.S.V.P.
Ms. Beth Holland
87 Grace Street
Richmond, Virginia 23223

Personal Invitations

Invitations to very small weddings and those to second marriages are often issued in the form of a personal note. Even though a bride is sending engraved invitations, she may, if she wishes, write personal ones to people to whom she feels especially close. This is the most flattering invitation possible. A typical note would read:

Dear Aunt Sally,

Dick and I are to be married at Christ Church on June tenth at four o'clock. We hope you and Uncle Jim will come to the church, and afterward to the reception at Greentree Country Club.

With much love from us both,

Jeanne

Insertions

Besides the invitations, several cards may be placed in the inner envelope (or outer envelope, if you omit the inner one). They all face the flap, and all are placed in front of the invitation itself—facing the person inserting them—or, if it is a folded invitation, within the fold.

Reception Invitations

When the guest list for the church is larger than that for the reception, a separate card is enclosed with the wedding invitation for those who are to be invited to the reception. The most commonly used form is:

> *Reception*
> *immediately following the ceremony*
> *Knoll's Country Club*
> *Lake Forest*
> *The favour of a reply is requested*
> *Lakeside Drive, Lake Forest, Illinois*

Invitations to the Reception Only

On some occasions the wedding ceremony is private, and a large reception follows. This frequently is the case in a second marriage. The invitation to the ceremony is given orally, and the wording of the reception invitation is:

> *Doctor and Mrs. John Huntington Smith*
> *request the pleasure of your company*
> *at the wedding reception*
> *of their daughter*
> *Ellen Marie Zimmerli*
> *and*
> *Mr. Gary Allan Peters*
> *Saturday, the first of November*
> *at half after twelve o'clock*
> *6 Linden Avenue*
> *Ringlewood*
> *R.s.v.p.*

When All Guests Go to Both Wedding and Reception

The cards illustrated above may also be used when every wedding guest is invited to go on to the reception, but it is more common to issue a combined invitation, as described on page 78.

When the reception follows a house wedding, or a ceremony in a hotel or club room, no separate invitation is necessary since all attending would be expected to stay on.

Pew Cards

Small cards with "Pew Number—" engraved on them may be enclosed with the invitations going to those family members and close friends who are to be seated in the reserved pews. The people receiving them take them to the church and show them to the ushers who escort them.

Similar cards are sometimes engraved "Within the ribbon," meaning that a certain number of pews are reserved for special guests but no specific pew is assigned.

Pew cards are often sent separately after the acceptances or regrets come in, so that the bride knows how many reserved pews will be needed and can assign the right number of seats.

Pew numbers were formerly sent on visiting cards, but today they must be written on a card (printed with the name of the bride and groom) that is large enough to meet postal regulations.

Admission Cards

Except when a wedding is held in a cathedral or a church that attracts sightseers, admission cards are not necessary. To ensure privacy in those circumstances, each guest is asked to present his or her card at the entrance. It is engraved in the same style as the invitation and reads:

Please present this card
at
The Washington Cathedral
Saturday, the tenth of June

"At Home" Cards

If you and your groom wish your friends to know what your new address will be, you may insert an "at home" card. These cards traditionally read:

At home [or, Will be at home]
after July twelfth
3842 Grand Avenue
Houston, Texas 77001

Many people receiving these cards, however, put them away, intending to enter them in an address book or file. Some time later they come across the card, only to find they cannot remember who will be at home at 3842 Grand Avenue after July twelfth. Therefore, even though you are not married at the time the invitation is sent, I recommend that your cards be engraved:

Mr. and Mrs. Brian Jamison
will be at home
(etc.)

This also provides an opportunity for the woman who plans to keep her own name to let her friends know. Her at-home card would read:

Janet Stock and David Burns
will be at home
(etc.)

Response Cards

It is regrettable that it is necessary to write these paragraphs, but the custom of enclosing response cards with wedding invitations is so widespread that it must be discussed.

The custom has arisen, I am afraid, out of sheer necessity. Too many people are lazy, thoughtless, or ignorant of good behavior and simply will not take the time or make the effort to answer invitations. When a caterer is hired, or the reception is held at a club or hotel, those in charge want to know the exact number of guests as soon as possible. While a rough estimate may be made from the quantity of invitations mailed, the more precise estimate must await the replies. Therefore, in an effort to get this information to the caterer in plenty of time, brides and their mothers often feel that the responses will arrive more quickly and surely if cards are enclosed.

While I thoroughly deplore the lack of appreciation shown by guests who would not otherwise bother to answer promptly, I am forced to accept the practicality of the cards in certain areas, or among certain groups where they have long been expected and accepted. If you have decided to include response cards, let them be most useful and in the best possible taste. Response cards are the smallest cards accepted by the postal service, engraved in the same style as the invitation. You may include self-addressed envelopes if you wish, preferably stamped. The cards should be in the following form:

M_____
_____accepts
_____regrets
Saturday, January fifth
Bristol Hotel
Abingdon

They should *not* include "number of persons_____" Those whose names appear on the outer and inner envelopes are the *only* ones invited, and other members of the family—children, especially—are not necessarily included. If you use the cards, each couple invited should receive a separate invitation, and the children or single people who are invited should receive their own invitations. When "number of persons" appears, people are inclined to think this means that other members of the family may attend, and you will find yourself with three times the number of guests you expect.

Invitation to a Belated Wedding Reception

When a reception is not held at the time of the wedding, the couple or their parents often have one later, possibly when the newlyweds return from their honeymoon. Although the party is held to celebrate the wedding, a true reception follows the ceremony, and the wording must be slightly changed.

Mr. and Mrs. Henry Matheson
request the pleasure of your company
at a reception
in honor of
Mr. and Mrs. Christopher Smith
(etc.)

A less formal invitation may be issued by using fill-in printed cards and writing "In honor of Doris and Christopher" or "In honor of Mr. and Mrs. Christopher Smith" at the top.

Announcements

Announcements are not obligatory, but in many cases they serve a useful purpose. They may be sent to those friends who are not invited to the wedding because the number of guests must be limited, or because they live too far away to make the journey. They may also be sent to acquaintances who, while not particularly close to the family, might still wish to know of the marriage. Announcements carry no obligation at all, so that many families send them rather than invitations to friends who are not expected to attend or to send a present. They are never sent to anyone who has received an invitation to the church or reception. Announcements are mailed as soon as possible after the wedding, preferably the next day. However, in the case of an elopement, or for some other reason, they may be mailed up to several months later.

Traditionally, announcements were always sent in the name of the bride's parents. The wording was as follows (and this is still perfectly correct):

Mr. and Mrs. Howard William Adams
have the honour of
announcing the marriage of their daughter
Katherine Leigh
to
Mr. Brian Charles Jamison
Saturday, the fifteenth of June
one thousand nine hundred and ninety-one
Briarcliff Manor, New York

There are several variations, equally correct. You may use "have the honour to announce," or merely the word "announce." The year is always included. The most formal wording is "one thousand nine hundred and ninety-one," but "nineteen hundred and ninety-one" is not incorrect.

However, I see no reason why today, when the attitude toward marriage is that it is a "joining" rather than a "giving" of a woman to a man, the announcements should not go out in both families' names. Although the privilege has always been accorded to the bride's family, it seems to me that when the parents of the groom are also proud and happy, it would be equally appropriate to have announcements sent in this way:

Mr. and Mrs. Howard William Adams
and
Mrs. Richard Curtis Jamison
announce the marriage of
Katherine Leigh Adams
and
Brian Charles Jamison
on . . .

Since announcements, unlike invitations, are intended to dispense information, surely the inclusion of the name of the groom's parents is informative as well as symbolic of their joy and approval.

The variations in circumstances, names, and titles follow those described previously for wedding invitations. For example, announcements for a young widow's or divorcée's second marriage are the same as for a first wedding:

Doctor and Mrs. Barry Farnham
and
Mr. and Mrs. Nigel Withers
announce the marriage of
Carolyn Farnham Flood
and
Nigel Withers, Junior
(etc.)

The announcement of the marriage of a widow of more mature years reads differently:

Mrs. George Saunders Simon
and
Mr. Craig Forsythe Douglas
announce their marriage
on Saturday, the fifth of April
one thousand nine hundred and ninety-one
at Vernon Valley
New Jersey

A divorcée and her new husband announce their marriage:

Mrs. Ann Rogers Duker
and
Mr. Peter Henwood Norton
announce their marriage
on Tuesday, the tenth of May
(etc.)

The bride who is an orphan and her bridegroom announce their marriage the same way, or, if the wedding was given by a relative or friend, the announcement, like the wedding invitation, begins with the names of those who hosted the wedding:

Mr. and Mrs. Thomas Allen Harrell
announce the marriage of
Miss Rosemary Londen
(etc.)

"At home" cards may be included with announcements.

Changes in Wedding Plans

When the Wedding is Canceled After Invitations Are Mailed

If the decision to cancel the wedding is a last-minute one, invited guests must be notified by telephone or telegram. If there is time, printed cards may be sent out:

Mr. and Mrs. Roy Lanza
announce that the marriage of
their daughter
Denise
to
Mr. Michael Newgaard
will not take place

Telegrams would read, "Regret to inform you wedding of Denise Lanza and

Michael Newgaard has been canceled." Or, to closer friends, "Regret that Denise's and Mike's wedding has been called off."

If the message is relayed by telephone, friends and relatives may be asked to help make the calls. It is easier for them to parry questions than it is for the bride or her mother, who are undoubtedly upset about the situation.

When the Wedding Date is Changed

When it is necessary to change the date of a wedding and the new date is decided upon after invitations have been printed but before they are mailed, it is not necessary for the bride to order new invitations. Instead, she may do one of three things:

> She may enclose a printed card, if there is time, saying, "The date of the wedding has been changed from March sixth to April twelfth."
> If the guest list is small, she may telephone the information or write a personal note.
> If the date is so soon that there is no possibility of having cards printed, she may neatly cross out the old date and insert the new one by pen.

When the wedding is postponed, not canceled, and there is time to have an announcement printed, it would read:

Mr. and Mrs. Clarence Scallion
regret that
owing to a death in the family [optional]
the invitations to
their daughter's wedding
on Saturday, December fifth
must be recalled

[or]

Owing to the death of
Mrs. Clarence Scallion
the marriage of her daughter
Ann
to
Mr. Kevin Denning
has been postponed

Most newspapers request announcement information at least three weeks before the wedding. The announcement generally appears the day following the ceremony. Since most newspapers receive more wedding announcements than they can print, the sooner yours is sent, and the more clear and concise the information, the better your chance of having it published.

Each paper will use as much of the information as it wishes, and in its own words. In general, you should provide the following:

- The bride's full name
- The bride's parents' name and town of residence
- Bride's parents' occupations
- Bride's maternal and paternal grandparents
- Bride's school and college
- Bride's occupation
- Groom's full name and town of residence
- Groom's parents' name and town of residence
- Groom's parents' occupations
- Groom's maternal and paternal grandparents
- Groom's school and college
- Groom's occupation
- Date of wedding
- Location of wedding and reception
- Names of bride's attendants and relationship to bride or groom, if any
- Names of groom's attendants and relationship to bride or groom, if any
- Description of bridal gown
- Description of attendants' gowns
- Name of minister or rabbi
- Name of soloist, if any
- Where couple will honeymoon
- Where couple will reside (town) after wedding

Kate's and Brian's announcement, which follows, is typical.

Miss Katherine Leigh Adams was married yesterday to Mr. Brian Charles Jamison. The marriage was performed at Village Lutheran Church, Briarcliff Manor, New York, by the Reverend Carol Vassallo.

The bride is the daughter of Mr. and Mrs. Howard Adams of Briarcliff Manor.

Her grandparents are Mr. and Mrs. Donald Adams of New York City and the late Mr. and Mrs. Clayton Horn of Boise, Idaho.

Mr. Jamison is the son of Mrs. Richard Jamison of Minneapolis, Minnesota, and the late Mr. Jamison. His grandparents are Mr. and Mrs. Dwight Jamison of Cross River, New York, and Mr. and Mrs. Bertrand Detweiler of Sarasota, Florida.

Mrs. Jamison wore an ivory gown of marquisette over silk and carried a bouquet of white roses, lilies of the valley, and stephanotis. Her long veil of Alençon lace had been worn by her mother and her grandmother.

Miss Lisa Adams served as her sister's maid of honor. The bridesmaids were Mrs. Paul Carvelas, a cousin of the bride; Miss Kathy Tognino; Miss Gay Evans and Miss Tina Votsis. Theresa Carvelas, daughter of Mr. and Mrs. Paul Carvelas, was flower girl. The bride's brother, Peter, served as ring bearer.

Mr. Jamison's best man was Thomas Coleman of Larchmont, New York. The ushers were Scott Jamison, a cousin of the groom; Michael Adams, brother of the bride; William Benson and Phillip Junggren. Junior ushers were Timothy Adams and Mark Jamison, brothers of the bride and groom.

Mrs. Jamison graduated from New York University and is a communications assistant for the National Broadcasting Company. Mr. Jamison graduated from the University of Minnesota and is associated with Moore Associates advertising agency in New York City.

After their wedding trip, the couple will live in New York City.

This completes the necessary requirements, with the exception of a description of the bridesmaids' gowns, included only when space permits.

A newspaper announcement of the wedding is also a way in which a bride who intends to keep her own name may make it known. In the second paragraph, following "The bride," she would have the newspaper add, "who will keep her own name." In the rest of the announcement, "Mrs. Jamison" would be changed to "the bride," or "Ms. Adams."

6

CLOTHES FOR THE BRIDAL PARTY

This chapter discusses in detail the clothing for every member of the bridal party. On pages 106–107 you will find a concise chart for handy reference, which will enable you to see at a glance the correct combination for every type of wedding.

The Bride's Costume

If you are a young bride being married for the first time, you are likely to choose a long white, or off-white, bridal gown. Whether you decide on a train or a long veil depends on the formality of your wedding and your own taste. If you are over forty, you may wear a long dress if you wish, but a pale pastel shade will be more becoming to your skin than white. Most mature brides do not wear a veil, and divorcées or widows being married for the second time definitely should not wear a veil. (See chapter 11.)

Kate Adams, who is young and being married for the first time in June—at a large formal wedding—chooses a dress of ivory marquisette over silk. Satin is traditional and correct for all seasons, but it is very hot in summer, and tulle, organdy, chiffon, cotton, and synthetics have largely taken its place from June through September. Velvet, brocade, and lace are all beautiful for winter weddings.

Kate's grandmother and mother had worn a beautiful veil of Alençon lace which they carefully preserved. Kate is delighted to wear it. It is draped gracefully

DRESS FOR BRIDAL PARTY AND GUESTS

	Most Formal Daytime	*Most Formal Evening*	*Semiformal Daytime*
Bride	Long white dress, train, and veil; gloves optional	Same as most formal daytime	Long white dress; short veil and gloves optional
Bride's attendants	Long dresses, matching shoes; gloves are bride's option	Same as most formal daytime	Same as most formal daytime
Groom, his attendants, bride's father or stepfather	Cutaway coat, striped trousers, pearl gray waistcoat, white stiff shirt, turndown collar with gray-and-black-striped four-in-hand or wing collar with ascot, gray gloves, black silk socks, black kid shoes	Black tailcoat and trousers, white pique waistcoat, starched-bosom shirt, wing collar, white bow tie, white gloves, black silk socks, black patent-leather shoes or pumps or black kid smooth-toe shoes	Black or charcoal sack coat, dove gray waistcoat, white pleated shirt, starched turndown collar or soft white shirt with four-in-hand tie, gray gloves, black smooth-toe shoes
Mothers and stepmothers of couple	Long or short dresses; hat, veil, or hair ornament; gloves	Usually long evening or dinner dress, dressy short cocktail permissible; veil or hair ornament if long dress; small hat, if short; gloves	Long or street-length dresses; gloves, head covering optional
Women guests	Street-length cocktail or afternoon dresses (colors are preferable to black or white); gloves; head covering optional	Depending on local custom, long or short dresses; if long, veil or ornament— otherwise, hat optional; gloves	Short afternoon or cocktail dress; head covering for church optional
Men guests	Dark suits; conservative shirts and ties	If women wear long dresses, tuxedos; if short dresses, dark suits	Dark suits

	Semiformal Evening	*Informal Daytime*	*Informal Evening*
Bride	Same as semiformal daytime	Short afternoon dress, cocktail dress, or suit	Long dinner dress or short cocktail dress or suit
Bride's attendants	Same length and degree of formality as bride's dress	Same style as bride	Same style as bride
Groom, his attendants, bride's father or stepfather	Winter, black tuxedo; summer, white jacket; pleated or piqué soft shirt, black cummerbund, black bow tie, no gloves, black patent-leather or kid shoes	Winter, dark suit; summer, dark trousers with white linen jacket or white trousers with navy or charcoal jacket; soft shirt, conservative four-in-hand tie; hot climate, white suit	Tuxedo if bride wears dinner dress; dark suit in winter, lighter suit in summer
Mothers and stepmothers of couple	Same as semiformal daytime	Short afternoon or cocktail dresses	Same length dress as bride
Women guests	Cocktail dresses, gloves, head covering for church optional	Afternoon dresses, gloves, head covering for church optional	Afternoon or cocktail dresses, gloves, head covering for church optional
Men guests	Dark suits	Dark suits; light trousers and dark blazers in summer	Dark suits
Groom's father or stepfather:	He may wear the same costume as the groom and his attendants, especially if he is to stand in the receiving line. If he is not to take part, however, and does not wish to dress formally, he may wear the same clothes as the men guests.		

over her head, mantilla fashion, and fastened securely underneath by clear combs sewn to the lace. Kate might also wear a face veil of tulle or net, but her long lace veil, which falls over her shoulders and down the length of the train, is better shown off without it.

Her shoes are of white peau de soie. Had her gown been satin, the shoes would have been of satin also. Kate's dress has long sleeves, so she may choose between short white gloves or none at all. Because she does not like the appearance of a glove with a finger removed or slit to allow the ring to be placed on her finger, Kate prefers to wear none.

She wears a string of pearls, given to her by Brian's mother, and pearl earrings, and she puts her engagement ring on her right hand. She should wear no other jewelry with colored stones, unless Brian has given her a pin or clip as a wedding gift.

Beth, who is being married during a semi-formal daytime wedding in October, is also wearing a long gown, but hers is of a very simple silk and satin blend. She is wearing a crescent of roses in her hair and carrying three white roses tied loosely with a satin ribbon. Her satin shoes are simple, unadorned pumps, and, like Kate, has chosen not to wear gloves. Beth is wearing a single pearl pendant at her neck, a wedding gift from Ben.

Susan and David are being married during an informal morning ceremony, followed by a brunch. Susan is wearing a short, peach colored silk dress, peach pumps, and is carrying a loose bouquet of creamy gardenias and camillias. She has chosen to wear nothing but a single flower in her hair and the gold bracelet David gave her as a wedding gift.

Borrowing a Wedding Dress

Often a friend or a relative is delighted to lend her wedding dress, particularly to someone she knows will take good care of it. There is no reason not to accept an offer of a loaned gown, as long as you indeed take extraordinarily good care of it and return it freshly cleaned and in perfect condition. If you do borrow a gown, you should show your appreciation with the loveliest gift you can give— preferably something for your friend's home, or a personal gift for her.

Renting a Dress

Many areas now have bridal and evening rental stores where a bride may rent her dress, just as the groom and ushers rent their costumes. If the dress is fresh, becoming, and in perfect condition, this can be a practical and satisfactory alternative to buying an expensive, one-time dress.

Mrs. Adams wisely suggests that Kate choose her bridesmaid's dresses without consulting each one first. She knows it is almost impossible to get four people to agree on one style and one color, so Kate chooses a model that is not too extreme, that will look well on any figure, and in a shade complementary to the coloring of each of the young women. Once she has chosen the style Kate invites her bridemaids to see what she has selected, or sends them a picture if they don't live locally. She asks each one for her size and then orders the dresses and arranges for fittings. She asks each bridesmaid to purchase her own shoes and to deliver them to her, if possible, so that she may have them dyed in a single lot. She suggests what jewelry will look best with the dresses, and she picks a floral head piece with a bit of tulle netting that will be most becoming to the hairstyles of the majority. She does not tell them how they must wear their hair.

Since the bridesmaids will pay for their own dresses, Kate thinks carefully about the cost of the gown she chooses. The dresses will all be of the same color, a soft dusty pink. The sprays the bridesmaids carry will be of a deeper pink mixed with white and rose. Kate's maid of honor will wear the same style as the bridesmaids but in a deeper shade, and her flowers will be different from those of the bridesmaids. The style of the dress is simple; a fitted bodice with long sleeves and a drop-waist skirt with a bow at the hip. The dresses must be one inch off the floor so that there is no chance of the bridesmaids tripping on the chancel steps.

Kate's four-year-old cousin is to serve as her flower girl. Her dress is of the same fabric and color as those of the bridesmaids, but it is made in a style more becoming to a little girl. She will carry a little basket of daisies rather than a spray of flowers, and will wear a pink satin bow at the back of her hair.

Kate's ring-bearer, her young brother, will wear a white linen suit with short pants and an Eton jacket. Long pants or replicas of the ushers' costumes are not in good taste for so young a child. The little boy's socks are white and so are his shoes. If Kate preferred that he wear a navy suit, he would wear dark knee socks and black shoes.

Considerations in Choosing Bridesmaids' Costumes

In addition to making sure that the gown she selects for her bridesmaids is basically flattering to each of the women in her bridal party, she also should consider whether it is in keeping with the style of her dress and that the color is appropriate to the season. They should be in the same degree of formality, the same length, and, to some extent the same style, as the bride's dress.

Remember backs! The back of the dress is of prime importance. Bridesmaids stand with their backs partially toward the guests as they watch the bride and groom at the altar or pulpit, and the congregation sees their backs as they go up and down the aisle. Therefore, some "back interest," such as bows, inserted panels and graceful lines are desirable.

The color is often chosen according to the season, with pale pastels especially nice in the spring and summer. The new trend of "black and white" weddings—particularly for formal evening ceremonies—is one which I feel is less appropriate than softer more traditional bridal party colors. If you choose to have a black and white wedding add color with bright bouquets. The more recent inclusion of printed fabrics in wedding party gowns adds a lovely garden party air, particularly for morning and afternoon weddings.

Consider the lighting for the ceremony when choosing colors for your wedding. If the site is quite dark, the lightest colors will stand out best. Blue is a bad choice for evening—candlelight tends to make it colorless. Dark browns and grays appear somber against the usual church or synagogue wood furnishings.

Bridesmaids may wear white, although it can detract from rather than add to the effect of the bride. If they do wear white, choose dresses with colored trim, or add very colorful flowers and accessories.

Gloves are optional. It really depends on how well they look with the gowns, and on the bride's preference. For an evening wedding with very formal dresses, full-length kid gloves are elegant and appropriate.

Head wear should be chosen with care. If your bridesmaids' dresses are Victorian or old-fashioned and yours is a daytime wedding, wide-brimmed hats can be charming. In most cases, however, a wreath, a band of artificial flowers, or a bow matching the color of the dresses is easier, more comfortable, and most becoming to everyone.

The Groom and His Attendants

Attire for the male members of the wedding party follows a definite pattern from which little deviation is permitted. In temperate climates, formal evening clothes mean a black tailcoat and matching trousers, stiff white shirt, wing collar, white tie, and white waistcoat.

Semiformal evening clothes means a black or midnight-blue dinner jacket (tuxedo) and matching trousers, piqué or pleated-front white shirt with attached collar, black bow tie, and black waistcoat or cummerbund. In hot weather a white dinner jacket and black cummerbund are used. Evening clothes should never be worn during the daytime.

Formal day clothes are appropriate for daytime weddings and should be worn whenever a wedding is scheduled before six o'clock. The daytime equivalent of the evening tailcoat is a black or Oxford-gray cutaway coat worn with black or gray striped trousers, pearl gray waistcoat, stiff white shirt, stiff fold-down collar, and four-in-hand black-and-gray tie or a dress ascot tie.

Less formal daytime clothes are the same except that a suit-style dark gray or black sack coat is substituted for the cutaway, the shirt is soft instead of stiff, and only a four-in-hand tie is worn. The Edwardian suit with its wide velvet lapels and a ruffled, often colored shirt is currently a popular costume. However, it looks just like that—a costume. The more conventional, simpler sack coat is in better taste.

In warm climates or very hot summertime in more northern climates, a formal daytime wedding is usually not attempted. In the informal wedding, although the bride may still wear a simple bridal gown, the men switch to lightweight suits or to dark gray or navy blue jackets with white trousers, white dress socks and white dress shoes, or black dress socks and black dress shoes. They

CUTAWAY   TAILCOAT   WAISTCOAT

may also wear white jackets with dark gray trousers. Shirts are soft white with attached collar, and ties should be four-in-hand with a dark, small, neat pattern.

Since her wedding is formal, Kate's bridegroom, Brian, his best man, and the ushers all wear cutaways. Their costumes are identical except that Brian and his best man may wear a tie of a different pattern, or they may wear ascots while the ushers wear four-in-hands. The cutaways or striped trousers may vary a touch in pattern, but the effect is one of uniformity.

Brian may send each usher specifications of what he will wear and ask him to rent the correct clothing. However, for the sake of uniformity, it is better if he writes and asks for their sizes, including their shoe sizes, and then orders the outfits himself from a rental agency. Shoes may be rented if everyone does not own the same dress shoes. The best man may take care of this task for the groom if it is convenient for him to do so. The attendants, in any case, pay the fee. In the past, ushers' gloves and ties were given to the attendants by the groom so he would know that they would match perfectly, but today formal wear rental

SACK COAT   TUXEDO

stores generally have these items in multiples in stock and they are part of the rental fee along with the rest of the clothing. Brian will provide his attendants' boutonnieres.

Brian and his best man will not wear gloves during the ceremony because of possible awkwardness in handling the ring, but the ushers will wear gloves from start to finish.

Since Beth and Ben are having a semiformal daytime wedding, Ben and his attendants are wearing charcoal sack coats, dove gray waistcoats, soft white shirts with four-in-hand ties, gray gloves, and black, smooth-toe shoes.

David and his attendants, for his and Susan's informal daytime wedding, are wearing dark suits, soft white shirts, and conservative four-in-hand ties. Because everyone in his wedding party owns a dark suit, white shirt and conservative tie, no rental arrangements need to be made.

If Brian and Ben have handled the rental of the clothes for themselves and their attendants, they are responsible for arranging for their return after the wedding. To do this each asks his best man, one of their ushers, or a friend who lives in the town where the wedding takes place to retrieve outfits from each person and take the clothes back to the store as soon as possible, usually the first weekday after the wedding, or the Saturday after a Friday wedding.

When the Groom is in the Service

If the groom is a member of the armed forces he has the option of being married in his uniform. If all his ushers were in the service, he would probably choose to do so, with his bride's agreement. If, however, some of his attendants were civilians, he would have a more difficult choice, since the harmonious appearance of the wedding would be spoiled. He would really be wiser to dress to conform to the civilians, since it cannot be the other way around.

When both members of the couple are in the service, the bride may also wear her uniform if she wishes, especially if they are married very suddenly or by a justice of the peace. In most cases, however, she would prefer to wear a more romantic wedding gown.

The Mothers of the Bride and the Groom

It is up to the mother of the bride to decide on the style and formality of her dress, although it is always courteous for her to discuss her thoughts with the mother of the groom before making a decision. As soon as she knows what she will wear, she should inform the groom's mother, who should choose a dress in a similar style. It is not essential that they be very much alike, but the receiving line will certainly present a more pleasing appearance if their dresses are of the same length and in complementary colors. In general, solid, pastel tones are the safest and most attractive for both women.

Even if one of the mothers is in mourning, she should not wear black for the wedding; she should choose a gray or lavender dress instead. In short, she should do nothing to impose her sadness on the happiness of the bridal couple.

The mothers of the bride and the groom leave their coats or stoles in the vestibule of the church or synagogue so as not to spoil the effect of their dresses. If the weather is cold, they may have their coats put at their seats ahead of time by an usher so that they can throw them over their shoulders during the ceremony should they become chilled.

If either the bride or the groom has a stepmother to whom they feel close and she will be at the wedding, it is thoughtful for the bride, once she knows what her own mother and her groom's mother are wearing, to pass this information along to the stepmother. This allows her to avoid dressing in an identical color, which would most likely prove embarrassing to both, and gives her a guideline as to the style and length of the dresses that the mothers are wearing.

The Fathers of the Bride and the Groom

Although it is not obligatory, the father of the bride should dress in the same style as the groom and his attendants. Since he will walk in the procession with the others, it makes a more unified effect if he dresses as they do. This would be true for any male escort of the bride should she not have a father or be estranged from her own father.

The groom's father also looks well when he dresses in the same fashion as the other men, but since he has no active part in the wedding, it is not so important, and he may dress as the guests do.

Both fathers wear boutonnieres. The bride's mother sometimes purchases her husband's, or they are given by the groom to both fathers.

If either the bride or the groom has a stepfather to whom they feel close and who will be attending the wedding, he may dress as the other guests do, or, if he is participating in any way in the ceremony, as the male members of the wedding party do.

The groom should make arrangements not only for his attendants, but for all fathers who will be dressing as the wedding party does. The groom should also be the one to discuss apparel with the stepfathers. If they elect not to dress identically to the wedding party, the bride and groom might make sure they have a boutonniere as a token of their happiness that the stepfathers are present.

7

PREWEDDING EVENTS

The weeks preceding the wedding are often filled with whirlwind rounds of parties and showers to honor the bride and groom.

Showers

Bridal showers traditionally are friendly gatherings of intimate friends, held to honor the bride and "shower" her with gifts. A new custom (which unfortunately has become widespread in recent years) of giving enormous parties—sometimes including every guest on the wedding list and sometimes including mere acquaintances who may never have met the bride—is in the poorest taste. These affairs are an obvious bid for booty and totally ignore the intimacy and friendship that are the charm of a true shower. The number of showers should be limited, to spare the bride's time and her friends' pocketbooks.

Though it is not so frequently done, there is no reason why the ushers or a close friend cannot give a shower for the groom. The theme would of course be masculine—a bar shower, a workshop shower, or a sports shower.

Who Gives the Showers?

Immediate members of your family—or your groom's—should *not* give you a shower. This includes your mothers, grandmothers, and sisters. Aunts, cousins, members of the bridal party, co-workers, or just friends are all eligible hostesses. There are exceptions. When a bride comes from a foreign country and knows no one here except her groom and his family, they may properly plan a shower. But ordinarily, for her immediate family to do so is in very poor taste.

Who Attends?

Members of both families, your attendants—including junior brides-maids—and close friends are invited to showers. The event is rarely a surprise, as it used to be, and in truth the hostess is wise to discuss the guest list with the .bride. By doing so, the bride who will be given several showers can divide her friends so that no one need go to too many showers or produce too many gifts.

The mother of the bride and, if she is nearby, the mother of the groom are usually included. If there are a great many showers, however, they need not be on every list. Other older people may be included too; relatives or family friends are flattered and happy to be a part of your festivities.

The majority of showers are given in the daytime, with the guest list composed of women. There is, however, an increasing trend toward mixed showers, held in the evening or on Sunday, to which your friends and their dates or husbands are invited. This type of shower, however, must be restricted to things that interest both the bride and the groom—for instance, a barbecue shower. A lingerie or bathroom shower would be distinctly out of place.

When a shower is given by a fellow worker or a member of a club to which you belong, it is perfectly all right for the hostess to ask only the office personnel or the members of the club.

Party Possibilities

Showers are held at any hour of the day, and they may range from a morning brunch to an after-dinner dessert. They may be brunches, coffees, luncheons, teas, cocktail parties, or just "showers." The list below includes traditional forms as well as some different ideas.

Brunch: Around 11 A.M. Menu consists of fruits such as melon and strawberries in summer or grapefruit and oranges in winter, a main course like scrambled eggs on artichoke bottoms, with crisp Canadian bacon, toast, brioche, croissants and butter, Danish pastries, coffee, and tea. Iced coffee is ideal in hot weather. Whatever the season, you may wish to serve Bloody Marys and white wine. Categories: household accessories or cleaning aids, spices and condiments, pantry items.

Coffee: Held in the morning. Simpler than brunch. Serve coffee, hot chocolate, bagels and lox or bacon and eggs, coffeecake, English muffins with marmalade or jam. Categories: cookbook, recipe, gardening.

Luncheon: From 12 to 2:30 P.M. May be sit-down or buffet. Menu can include white wine and/or wine cassis, filet of sole wrapped in lettuce leaves and poached in a white wine sauce, rice pilaf, and tossed green salad in winter; or cold poached salmon, steamed new potatoes, and asparagus vinaigrette in summer. Strawberry sherbet and lacy cookies make a fine dessert at any time of year. Categories: lingerie, bathroom, bedroom, kitchen.

Tea: Rather more ceremonial than morning parties. Very thin sandwiches, canapés, fruit tarts, chocolate cake, and petits fours are served with hot or iced tea, depending on the season. Categories: kitchen, round-the-clock, paper, linen, bedroom.

Cocktail party: Six o'clock or Sunday noon. Offer cocktails, white and red wine, and a nonalcoholic punch, bite-size seafood quiche, prosciutto wrapped around melon or fresh figs, miniature tart shells filled with ratatouille, and raw vegetables with a curry mayonnaise, or a sausage in brioche, a cheese board with assorted breads and crackers, olives, and nuts. Categories (to please the groom): bar, barbecue, or, if he is interested, gardening.

Dessert shower: 7:30 P.M. May be for women only or may include men. Menu consists of white wine and punch, chocolate cake, raspberry Bavarian cream, open fruit tart, assorted cookies, tea and coffee. Cold drinks are served later in the evening. Categories (if women only): same as luncheon or tea. If men are invited, same as cocktail party.

Special Showers

A *pantry shower* means a gift of food for your kitchen cupboard, not glassware or china. Canned goods, prepared foods, and gourmet specialties qualify.

Lingerie showers are for women only. Any item of lingerie is acceptable, and occasionally the guests chip in to buy the bridal nightgown and robe. The bride's size and color preferences should be noted on the invitations.

A *round-the-clock shower* means that a certain hour of the day is written on each guest's invitation. She brings a gift appropriate to that hour—for example, a dustpan and brush for "10 A.M." or cocktail glasses for "6 P.M."

A *gardening shower* means not only tools, gloves, and equipment but bulbs, seeds, and plants that can be planted outside. For an apartment dweller it could also mean items for a window garden or terrace.

At a *recipe shower* each guest brings her favorite recipe and a small gadget to be used in the making. This is ideal for a "proxy shower" when the bride lives out of town and cannot attend, because the recipes and gadgets are so easy to mail.

A *paper shower* might well include plastics. Paper flowers, table mats, monogrammed napkins or book matches, a magazine subscription, possibly a check from your mother, are welcome gifts.

The more widely known showers, such as kitchen or linen, need no explanation.

Invitations

Invitations are always informal and are usually written on the illustrated cards found at every stationer's. They are attractive and allow space for all the details you need to include. The inner page looks something like this:

> Kind of shower *Kitchen (red and white)*
> Where *At Jessica Woods' 12 Oak Street*
> When *Saturday, May 7, at noon*
> For *Bonnie Findlay*
>
> R.s.v.p. *(555-5454)*

It is most important that the hostess provide the guests with the necessary information about colors, sizes, and styles—so helpful to them as well as to the bride.

Invitations may also be in the form of a note including the same details, or issued by telephone. Since showers are informal affairs, engraved invitations are unnecessary. The information may, however, be written in hand on the hostess's notepaper.

Decorations

Decorations are almost always in keeping with the theme of the shower. At Kate's kitchen shower, for example, the hostess used copper teapots of flowers as decorations, and fruits and vegetables arranged as a centerpiece. Containers for the gifts, too, are in keeping with the theme. A laundry basket, dressed up with colored ribbons, makes a fine receptacle for bathroom shower gifts, and a wheel-barrow would be ideal for a garden shower. The centerpiece for the table may be a fresh-flower arrangement, or it may be a cake, decorated with white or pastel icing. The gifts themselves, attractively arranged with garlands of flowers or piled in a pretty container, such as a colorful parasol, may also provide the main table decoration.

A Wishing Well

Many shower invitations carry a note saying "wishing well." This means the guests bring an additional gift of very little value but of great use to the bride in setting up her household. A role of paper towels, a bottle of dish detergent, a dishcloth—anything of that sort is placed, unmarked, into a replica of a well. Sometimes an amusing poem or saying is tied to the gift, which may or may not be wrapped.

The Gifts

Years ago, shower presents were invariably handmade with loving care: a true token of affection. Today few of us have time to devote to such projects, but we can still take great pains with the selection and presentation of our gifts.

Aside from the fact that one must give something appropriate to the type of shower, the choice is limited only by the guest's taste and her pocketbook. Shower gifts do not take the place of a wedding gift and should be neither so expensive nor so elaborate. Money is of no importance—it is the thought or effort behind the gift which gives it its value.

Occasionally a hostess will limit the price range of the gifts by writing, for instance, "under $20 please" on the invitation. This is permissible, perhaps, when she fears that one or two guests may bring a gift that will make others suffer by comparison, but it is not in the best of taste. And in no circumstances should the hostess ever tell a guest to bring a specific item.

Gifts are taken to the shower by the guests. If a friend cannot accept, she is not obligated to send a gift, but since a shower guest is generally a close friend or family member, she will undoubtedly want to do so. She sends the gift to the hostess's house ahead of time, so that it may be opened with the other presents.

A card should be enclosed with each gift, so that Kate need not keep asking "Who gave this?" as she opens the package. If one has a personal visiting card, it is correct to enclose it in a gift. Equally correct are the charming little shower-gift cards provided by gift shops.

The gifts may be wrapped either by the donor or by the store where they are purchased, generally in the most "bridey" wrappings possible. But if the hostess is planning a special arrangement or manner of presentation, she may ask that the guests drop their presents off at her home a day or two ahead of time. She then adds uniform or coordinated outer wrappings to achieve the effect she wishes.

Opening Gifts

The moment at which the bride opens her gifts is determined by the kind of shower. At a coffee or tea they may be opened before the food is served. At a "dessert" they would surely be opened later. At a cocktail party the couple opens the presents as soon as all the guests have arrived—while cocktails are being enjoyed.

Kate sits in a spot where everyone has room to group around her and watch. The hostess provides a big receptacle for the wrappings, and one of the guests—in this case Lisa, as maid of honor—keeps a list of the gifts and the donors. As each present is unwrapped, Kate thanks the one who gave it, and it is passed around for everyone to have a closer look. She must try to show her enthusiasm for each present, and should duplicates appear, she should be ready to make light of it or explain how much more useful she knows a "pair" would be.

This opening ceremony is all the entertainment that is necessary. Unless the hostess has a most unusual idea, or one which she knows her guests are dying to try, she should not suggest games or organized pastimes. A shower should not last more than two hours (except for a luncheon or evening party, which might last two and a half to three), and the gift opening, refreshments, and a few minutes to relax and chat will more than fill the time.

The Bride's Thanks

The bride's sincere personal thanks at the time she opens her gifts are quite sufficient. The weeks and days before the wedding are an incredibly busy time for her, and she often has all she can do to keep up with the obligatory wedding-gift thank-yous. Many brides do wish to show their appreciation by a note, however, and of course it is not incorrect in any way, but it is not necessary. Naturally, when a friend who cannot attend the shower sends a gift, she should receive a thank-you note immediately.

The Bridesmaids' Luncheon

The bridesmaids' luncheon is a lovely but optional tradition. It may be given by the bridesmaids for the bride, or it may be given by the bride for her bridesmaids. It is not a shower, although it is the occasion when the bride gives her attendants her gifts to them, and they their joint gift to her. If there is no bridesmaids luncheon, these gifts would be given at the rehearsal dinner. It is much like any other luncheon—an occasion, really, for good friends to get together and chat for the last time before one of the group leaves, or at least changes her status.

In Kate Adams' case, two of her attendants are giving showers for her, so she decides to repay their kindness with a luncheon for the group. The party takes place at home, on the Saturday before the wedding. Unfortunately, one of Kate's bridesmaids, a friend from college, will not yet have arrived from North Carolina.

Kate and her mother prepare a light but delicious luncheon—gazpacho, crabmeat crepes with a Mornay sauce, watercress salad, raspberry tarts, white wine, coffee and tea. They make plans in advance to change the menu to a cold poached salmon with green dill sauce if the weather is very hot.

Mrs. Adams bakes a cake, and Kate decorates it with white icing, pink candy flowers, and garlands of pale green leaves. The table is covered with a white cloth, the napkins are pink, and there are tiny containers of fresh pink roses at each place. Since the Adamses have a lovely dining room, Kate chooses to have the luncheon seated. The guests serve themselves from the dishes arranged on the sideboard and take the places indicated by pink bordered place cards. Had Kate wanted to have lunch on the patio, she would have served the meal buffet style from the dining room table and seated her guests at tables set up outside.

After the bridesmaids are settled, Kate gives them their gifts. She has given them all pearl earrings, knowing who has pierced ears and who doesn't, which they can wear during the wedding. The bridesmaids also have a gift ready for Kate, a small silver tray with their first names, in their own handwriting, etched on it.

Kate serves the wine, making a toast of thanks to her attendants, and the maid of honor reciprocates with wishes for her happiness.

After lunch the women have coffee and tea on the terrace, and the party ends. The bridesmaids go off for the final fittings on their dresses, and Kate goes upstairs to get a moment's rest and catch up with her thank-you notes.

Different circumstances call for different plans. Because most of her attendants are from out of town and not able to make a trip the week before her wedding, Beth gives a luncheon for them on the day of her wedding. This gives them a chance to relax together before they begin dressing for the ceremony and the arrival of the photographer to take his first pictures. Beth's mother, having helped her daughter prepare the luncheon which will be served on their deck, has also invited Ben's parents to join her and Mr. Newberry for lunch, giving them a chance to get to know one another a little better before all the rush of the wedding festivities begin. After lunch, Mrs. Newberry invites Mrs. Clark to accompany her to the country club to put placecards on the bridal table and to check that everything has been arranged as requested.

The Bachelor's Dinner

Bachelor dinners are not held as often as they used to be, especially when ushers come from far away and frequently arrive just in time for the rehearsal the day before the wedding. These dinners are often frowned on by the bride, who has heard what dreadful orgies they're supposed to be, and at other times the groom simply does not want to go to the expense of another party.

Actually, the "orgy" is more fiction than fact. Even years ago, the height of the celebration was the breaking of the glasses with which the men drank a toast to the bride. Today, when a bachelor dinner is held, it is simply a dinner attended by men in the groom's wedding party, his father, any brothers or other relatives, and other male friends.

Discussion generally ranges from talk about sports to philosophical thoughts about marriage, and at some point during the dinner, the groom takes the opportunity to toast his bride. He may also give his gifts to his attendants at this dinner or, if one is not held, at the rehearsal dinner. Brian's gift to his ushers is a slim leather card case marked with their initials. To his best man he gives a leather-covered decanter monogrammed with the best man's initials.

The groom himself may give the bachelor dinner or his father may arrange it. This dinner may also be planned by the best man and the ushers. It should be held several days before the wedding so that it will not interfere with the rehearsal dinner and so that if it runs very late, the groom and his attendants will be able to catch up on their rest before the wedding. While it may be held at the groom's home if he or his father is giving it or at the home of one of his attendants if they are giving it, it more generally takes place in a club or a restaurant.

Parties for Out-of-Town Guests

When many guests are traveling from out of town for your wedding and are not able to be included in the invitation to the rehearsal dinner, you may be concerned that they are entertained in some way. A very thoughtful offer is sometimes made by a friend to give a party for these guests while the wedding party and the bride's and groom's parents are busy at the rehearsal and rehearsal dinner. The parents of one of Kate's bridesmaids offer this for Kate's and Brian's visiting guests, and Kate's aunt arranges an informal luncheon and swimming party for the out-of-towners on the day of the wedding, thereby relieving Kate, her mother and Brian's mother of the obligation to entertain them instead of resting and preparing for the wedding.

These parties are almost always informal. They may be picnics, barbecues or cookouts, or fireside buffets in cooler weather. In addition to the out-of-town guests, the guest list includes close friends of the bride and her parents. Naturally the bride, groom, and their parents are invited. They may stop in to share a few moments with friends, but are not expected to stay for long.

Because David's and Susan's wedding is in the late morning, they feel no obligation to have out-of-town guests entertained, assuming rightly that they will be happy to sleep a little later than usual, have breakfast, and dress at a leisurely pace. Susan's daughter has extended an invitation to any guests staying over a second night to attend an informal buffet. Although David and Susan will have departed on their honeymoon, many of the guests are friends with one another and will enjoy this opportunity to spend more time together in a comfortable setting.

Pre-Wedding Luncheon

A friend or relative often gives a small luncheon for the bridal party on the day of a late afternoon or evening wedding. This can be a tremendous help to the bride's family since it relieves them of the responsibility of entertaining the attendants during the hours before the wedding. In Ben's and Beth's case, Mrs. Newberry's closest friend invites the bride and groom, their attendants, Ben's son and daughter, and the Newberrys and the Clarks. Beth and Ben arrive with their own families and depart as soon as lunch is over to rest and to allow ample time for dressing. The bridesmaids and ushers linger a while longer, and leave in time to be ready at the appointed hour.

There is an old superstition that the bride and groom should not see each other on the day of the wedding until they meet at the ceremony. Few of us worry about those old wives' tales any more, however, and this wedding day luncheon relieves nervous tension for some brides and grooms, and fills the hours happily. Other couples prefer to avoid any social commitments earlier on the wedding day, and still others prefer a quiet lunch with their families or their own attendants.

The Rehearsal

In order to ensure that your ceremony goes smoothly and is dignified and beautiful, it is essential that you, your groom, and all the participants attend the rehearsal and pay the strictest attention.

The groom's parents, who have no active part in the ceremony, may attend if they wish, but it is not necessary unless the groom's father is serving as his best man. They may prefer to use the time for last-minute preparations for the rehearsal dinner.

All participants should arrive on time, take the instructions of the minister or rabbi seriously, and listen attentively. They should also dress appropriately and behave respectfully for being in a house of worship.

In addition to instruction from the minister or rabbi, this is the time for any special instructions for ushers from the bride and the groom. In the case of Kate's and Brian's wedding, guests of both families are fairly equal in number. If this were not the situation, the ushers might be instructed to fill in the groom's side of the church or synagogue with guests of the bride's family which were nearly twice in number. This would also be the time for Brian to name a head usher, if there is to be one, to be in charge of all the other ushers and make any required decisions, and to confirm which ushers will escort the mothers of the bride and groom. (See Chapter 8 for more details on correct procedures for ushers.)

It used to be considered bad luck for the bride to take part in her own rehearsal, so for many years she often sat by and watched her part played by a stand-in. Today, however, most ministers and rabbis prefer that the bride and groom take their own places and go through the motions themselves, in order to make the service as flawless as possible. No words of the actual ceremony are said at this time, although the minister or rabbi may state what will be said and when.

The organist should be present so that the pace and spacing can be decided upon. The attendants form the procession and practice the walk up the aisle. The minister or rabbi instructs each member on where to stand, and the bride should carry a simulated bouquet to practice handing it to her maid of honor and retrieving it again at the end of the ceremony. Often at a shower, a guest will decorate a paper plate with ribbons from the gifts, or make a "bouquet" of ribbons for the bride to have to carry during the rehearsal.

Occasionally a minister or rabbi will ask the wedding party to go through the ceremony quickly a second time, to be sure everyone is confident about what he or she is supposed to do. At the conclusion of the rehearsal, the manner of pairing and forming the recessional is determined.

The Rehearsal Dinner

Although she is traveling from Minnesota to New York, Brian's mother insists on giving the rehearsal dinner following the rehearsal, the evening before the wedding. This is not obligatory, but it is a custom that is becoming more and more widely accepted. Mrs. Jamison feels that this is little enough repayment for the courtesy and hospitality that Kate's family has shown her and that she knows will continue over the weekend of the wedding.

Mrs. Jamison writes or calls Mrs. Adams to discuss it. She asks for the names and addresses of the family members who should be included, and gets the same information about the bridal party from Kate and Brian. She asks Mrs. Adams to reserve a room for the party at the country club, or, if that is not available, at an attractive hotel or restaurant nearby. When she receives word of the location, she writes to the manager and confirms the reservation. She gives an estimate of the probable number of guests, and the manager replies, discussing the arrangements and costs. Mrs. Jamison sends the invitations two to three weeks before the wedding. She uses her notepaper and writes the necessary information by hand. She could equally well write personal letters, but the guest list is quite long, and the notes are more quickly done.

The list includes the bridal party, Kate's and Brian's parents, the husbands, wives, fiancé(e)s and live-in companions of their attendants, grandparents, and Brian's favorite aunt and uncle who are making the trip from Wisconsin. The minister or rabbi may be invited, so Brian's pastor who was requested by his mother to perform the ceremony is invited. Since the bridal party is large, it is decided not to include other relatives or out-of-towners. In any case, as mentioned before, a party is being given for other visitors.

As soon as Mrs. Jamison arrives in New York—on the Thursday before the wedding—she goes to the club and makes more specific plans as to the seating, parking facilities, and other details, and she confirms the menu. The following afternoon, when the tables are set up, she checks on the decorations and the table arrangement and positions the place cards.

Brian's mother has decided on a U-shaped table, which allows everyone to have a sense of being seated together. Kate will sit on Brian's right at the outside center of the base of the U. Her maid of honor sits on Brian's left, his best man on Kate's right. The attendants sit on either side, alternating bridesmaids and

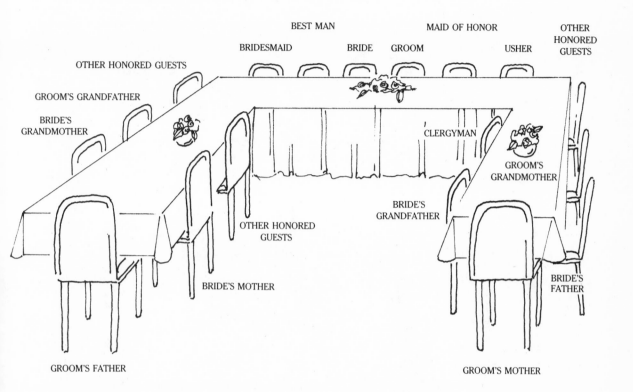

The rehearsal dinner is generally given by the groom's family and is as elaborate or as simple as they wish. This diagram suggests an arrangement for a good size party. For a larger party, simply extend the arms of the U to accommodate more guests. The overriding consideration is to arrange the seating so that dinner partners will be most congenial to everyone.

ushers as shown by the placecards. Mrs. Jamison, as hostess, sits at one end of the U and Brian's uncle at the other end. Were Mr. Jamison to be living, he would sit at the end where Brian's uncle will be sitting. Mrs. Adams sits on Brian's uncle's right, and Kate's grandmother on his left. Mr. Adams sits on Brian's mother's right, and Kate's grandfather sits on her left. Kate's other grandparents and Brian's grandparents are seated, as are the other guests, along both sides of the arms of the U, in whatever order seems to be most congenial to everyone.

If the space were such that only a rectangular table were possible, the bride and groom would sit at the center of one long side, the bridal party beside and across from them, the groom's parents at each end and the other guests between. The guests of honor would take the same places as described above.

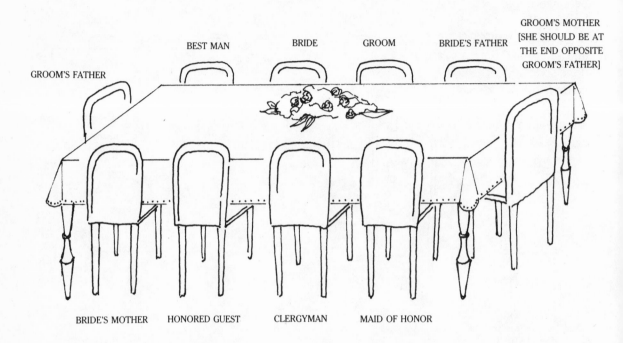

BEST MAN   BRIDE   GROOM   BRIDE'S FATHER

GROOM'S MOTHER
[SHE SHOULD BE AT
THE END OPPOSITE
GROOM'S FATHER]

GROOM'S FATHER

BRIDE'S MOTHER   HONORED GUEST   CLERGYMAN   MAID OF HONOR

When a rectangular table is used for a rehearsal dinner, the bride and groom are seated on one long side and face their bridal party with family members all around.

The dinner starts with a short cocktail hour, allowing the two families to chat with the attendants and to get to know each other slightly. A pianist plays softly at one end of the room, and he asks the bride and groom and others for their requests.

Dinner is announced after half an hour, the guests find their seats quickly, and the meal is served. The menu consists of shrimp cocktail, roast rack of lamb, eggplant, zucchini and tomato au gratin, roasted potatoes, green salad with herb vinaigrette dressing, peach melba, coffee, and tea. As soon as it is served, the waiters fill glasses with champagne and Mrs. Jamison, as hostess, makes the first toast. She welcomes the guests and makes a remark or two about her happiness at the coming marriage.

Kate's father makes a toast in return, saying how delighted the Adamses are, and this is followed by toasts given by any or all of the ushers, relatives, and bridesmaids.

Since the rehearsal dinner is somewhat informal, the toasts need not be too serious or sentimental, as they are on the wedding day. They should, of course, be sincere and happy but—especially for those given by the ushers—a bit of humor is in order.

When everyone who can possibly think of anything to say has said it, Kate and Brian take the opportunity to thank their attendants and, if they have not done so at an earlier party, give them their presents. If arrangements have been made for dance music, Kate and Brian lead the way to the dance floor, and all those who feel like dancing follow. The music and dancing are not essential, and are usually not included so as not to make too long an evening of partying the night before the wedding, but Mrs. Jamison felt that it would add to the happiness of the evening.

8

THE WEDDING CEREMONY

The wedding day begins early, with great excitement and the feeling of butter-flies in everyone's stomachs. No matter how carefully the preparations have been made, there are always last-minute arrangements to make and crises to be solved. The hours fly. There is never enough time—for anyone that is, except the bride and groom. With their chores all completed, and everyone trying to protect them from the confusion and relieve them of responsibilities, for them the day crawls by.

The Hour Approaches

At one-thirty, Kate and Brian, whose ceremony is scheduled for four-thirty, leave the luncheon given for their wedding party. Kate goes to her house to finish last-minute packing, to rest, and at three to bathe and start to dress. Brian and his family are staying at a motel nearby, and he goes there to relax by the pool until it is time to get ready.

The bridesmaids arrive at three o'clock at Kate's house, where some will dress in the guest room, and others will dress in the den. They could change in a room in the church, at their homes, or at the various places where they are staying, but Kate feels that she will be less nervous if she sees them leave together at the proper moment. Also, she knows that having them with her will keep her from worrying about possible mishaps and add to her own enjoyment.

As Kate emerges from her room, one of the bridesmaids asks if Kate has

"Something old, something new, something borrowed, and something blue," and she remembers that she has forgotten to put on the blue garter her attendants had given her at the bridesmaids' luncheon. She is wearing a string of pearls given her as a wedding present by Brian's mother, her veil belonged to her mother and her grandmother before her, and she has borrowed a lace handkerchief to complete the requirements. Someone also remembers that she should have a "sixpence in her shoe," and her father produces the acceptable substitute—a new penny.

The bridesmaids receive their bouquets, which have been delivered to Kate's house, along with the bride's bouquet, the corsages for Kate's mother and grandmother, and the flower girl's basket.

The Bridal Party Goes to the Church

The little flower girl, who has dressed at Kate's house with her mother, one of Kate's attendants, has loved being a part of the excitement and flurry of activity. The ring bearer, who has been dressed at his own home, arrives, and it is time for the party to go to the church. Four limousines are waiting. Mrs. Adams goes in the first, accompanied by the two small children. Two bridesmaids go in the next, and the other two, with the maid of honor, in the third. Although the bridesmaids could all fit into one limousine, they would be somewhat cramped, and Kate feels that they will be more comfortable, and their dresses less crushed, if they go in two cars. Kate and her father will go in the last car, allowing just enough time to arrive a minute or two before the appointed hour. This car will remain at the church entrance to take Kate and Brian from the church to the reception. Mr. Adams will return in the car with Mrs. Adams and the children.

If Kate did not wish to hire limousines or felt it was an unnecessary expense, she would ask close friends and relatives to provide cars. Young men friends who are not included in the wedding party are generally delighted to serve as chauffeurs.

The Ushers Go to the Church

Meanwhile, the ushers dress wherever they are staying and make their own way to the church, arriving forty-five minutes to an hour before the ceremony. The best man or the head usher should make sure that they all have transportation, and the head usher is responsible for seeing that they arrive on time.

The head usher assigns the others their posts. Those who are most likely to recognize family members and close friends—brothers of the bride and groom, for instance—should be given the center aisle. He also designates which ones will be responsible for rolling out the white carpet and laying the ribbons along the ends of the pews.

Several front pews on each side of the center aisle are reserved for immediate members of the family and sometimes for a few closest friends. The people who are to sit there are usually notified by a pew card (see chapter 5) or by word of mouth. Even if one family, as in Brian's case, comes from a distance and may have very few guests attending, the same number of pews are reserved on each side. Rather than three on his side and seven on Kate's, five on each side are reserved, and the ushers are told that after the first three pews are filled by the most immediate family, other guests with "within the ribbon" cards may be evenly distributed on both sides. These pews are called "within the ribbon" because the ribbon that is laid over the ends of the pews to keep people from leaving too quickly starts at the last reserved pew and runs to the back of the church.

When an usher recognizes someone he thinks should be seated in the reserved pews but who fails to present a card, he may ask, "Do you have a pew card?" This should not be necessary, however, as guests are supposed to hand them to the usher without being asked. When the guest has no card, the usher asks which side he or she would like to sit on, the bride's or the groom's. Then he finds the guest the best vacant seat on that side. The left side of the church, from the back is the bride's; the right, the grooms'. At weddings where the great majority of guests are friends of one family or the other, he may ask some of them if they would mind sitting on the other side. This not only makes the congregation look more balanced but offers more guests the desirable seats near the aisle, and closer to the altar.

The ushers and guests do not walk in stony silence. They exchange a few casual remarks about the weather, mutual friends, or whatever, and the guest may thank the usher for finding the seat. Men, especially tall men, should offer the aisle seat to the women they are accompanying and should enter the pew first to avoid climbing past them.

Seating Divorced Parents

When the bride's parents are divorced but have remained on friendly terms, both of them—and, if they have remarried, both stepparents—will attend the wedding and the reception. The bride's mother and stepfather sit in the front pew on the left side of the aisle. Members of her mother's immediate family—grandparents, aunts, and uncles—sit immediately behind them. The bride's father, after escorting his daughter up the aisle and presenting her to her groom, sits in the next pew back with his wife and their family members.

If there is bitterness between the divorced parents but the bride has remained close to both, the situation is infinitely more difficult. Unless she has lived with her father since the divorce, her mother gives the wedding. Her father gives her away and sits in the pew behind his ex-wife's family. His second wife may sit there too, if the bride wishes, but if her mother strongly resents the new wife, the latter would be more tactful to sit farther back in the church with a member of her family or a friend. In these circumstances, the father may not even attend the reception. Grandparents and other relatives on his side may be excluded entirely.

In the event that the wedding is given by the bride's father, the seating arrangement remains the same. The bride's mother, and her present husband, if the bride approves, sit in the first pew. Only when the bride has lived with her father and stepmother, and has had little to do with her own mother, do her father and stepmother sit in the front pew. Ordinarily, the father's family sits in the second or third pew, where he joins them after escorting his daughter.

When the groom's parents are divorced, they are seated in the same manner. His mother, accompanied by the members of her family who are closest to her, sits in the first pew on the right side of the aisle. His father and family sit in the next pew behind the groom's mother's family.

The Last Few Minutes

Brian and his best man arrive at the church about fifteen minutes before the hour of the ceremony. They enter by a side door and wait in the minister's study or in a side room until they receive the signal to enter the church.

Mrs. Jamison arrives at the church five to ten minutes before the wedding is to start and waits in the vestibule. Kate's mother has already arrived. When the rest of the wedding party is assembled, Mrs. Jamison is escorted to the front pew on the right by her nephew, who is an usher. Were her husband to be alive, he would follow right behind them. Rather than sitting alone, Mrs. Jamison has asked her brother and his wife, Brian's favorite uncle and aunt, to sit with her in the first pew.

Mrs. Adams is then escorted to the front pew on the left by her son, Michael, who is an usher.

A white canvas carpet, rolled or folded at the foot of the chancel steps, is picked up by the two junior ushers and carefully drawn back the length of the aisle. A broad white ribbon, as mentioned before, is put in place on each side of the aisle at the last moment. These ribbons are folded on the ends of the last reserved pews, and as soon as Mrs. Adams is seated and the carpet in place, the two ushers who have been assigned to do so walk with the ribbons to the back of the church, laying them over the end of each row. They are not removed until the guests in the reserved pews leave the church, enabling them to get away quickly before the rest of the guests can move.

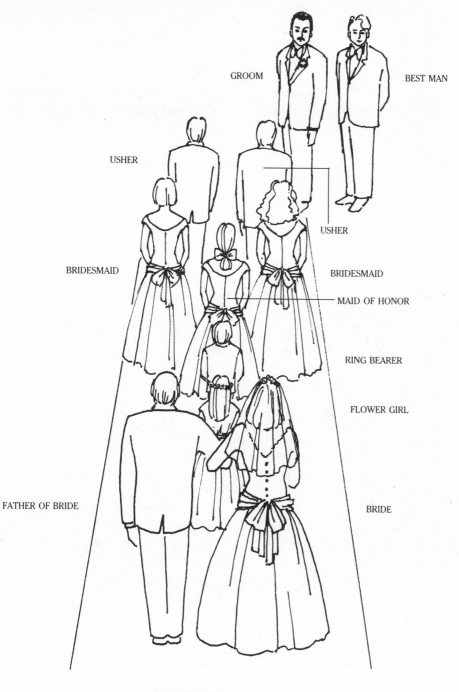

GROOM

BEST MAN

USHER

USHER

BRIDESMAID

BRIDESMAID

MAID OF HONOR

RING BEARER

FLOWER GIRL

FATHER OF BRIDE

BRIDE

CHRISTIAN PROCESSIONAL

After the bride's mother is taken to her place, no guest may be seated from the center aisle. If people arrive after that, they must stand in the vestibule, go to the balcony, or slip into a back pew from the side aisle.

The bride and her father arrive at the precise moment for the wedding to start, and the procession forms in the vestibule. As soon as the attendants have taken their places, a signal is given, and the minister, followed in order by the groom and the best man, enters the church. Many churches have a buzzer system to announce that all is ready; in others the sexton or wedding coordinator goes to the vestry with the message; sometimes the opening bars of the wedding march or another specific piece of music give the signal. In any case, the groom and best man take their places at the right side of the aisle, or in some churches, they stand at the top of the steps to the chancel. The best man stands to the groom's left and slightly behind him, and they both face the congregation. As soon as they reach their places, the procession starts.

The Ceremony Itself

The ushers lead the procession, walking two by two, the shortest men first. Junior ushers follow the adults. Junior bridesmaids, if there are any, come next. The bridesmaids follow, usually walking in pairs also. When there are very few bridesmaids, or an uneven number, they may walk in single file. After the bridesmaids comes the maid or matron of honor. Should there be both, the maid of honor walks closer to the bride. A flower girl and finally a ring bearer (if they are included in the party) immediately precede the bride, who walks on her father's right. The spaces between each couple or individual should be even—approximately four paces long. The "hesitation step," which used to be very popular, is now considered awkward and difficult, a slow, natural walk is safest and prettiest.

The arrangement of the attendants at the front of the church varies. Kate and Brian prefer that the ushers and junior ushers divide as they reach the chancel steps, so that three men stand on either side. The pairs of bridesmaids also separate and stand in front of the ushers. In some churches, the ushers line up on one side and the bridesmaids on the other, or, if the arrangement works out better, they stand in front of or up in the chancel in front of the choir stalls rather than on the steps. This is a question on which Kate and Brian asked their pastor's advice, since his years of experience have shown him what makes the most attractive picture. Kate's and Brian's attendants form their lines sloping outward so that they may all be seen from the pews.

The maid of honor stands at Kate's left and below or behind her. The best man remains in the same position he was in, but he is now on Brian's right, since

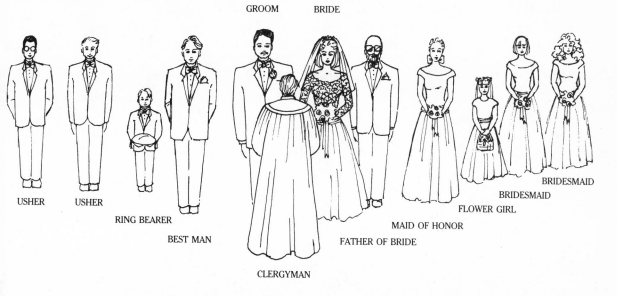

GROOM   BRIDE

USHER   USHER

RING BEARER

BEST MAN

CLERGYMAN

FATHER OF BRIDE

MAID OF HONOR

FLOWER GIRL

BRIDESMAID

BRIDESMAID

CHRISTIAN CEREMONY, AT THE ALTAR

they turned to face the altar as Kate and her father arrive at the steps. The flower girl stands behind the maid of honor, and the ring bearer stands behind the best man.

When the bride reaches the groom's side, she let's go of her father's arm, transfers her flowers to her left arm, and gives her right hand to her groom. He puts it through his left arm, and her hand rests near his elbow. If Kate is not comfortable this way, they may stand hand in hand or merely side by side. The minister faces them from the top of the steps.

As it is a Protestant ceremony, Kate's father remains by her side or a step or two behind, until the minister says, "Who gives this woman to be married?" Kate's father reaches in front of her and puts her right hand into that of the pastor and says, "I do." In some ceremonies the bride's father says, "Her mother and I do." Then he turns and joins Mrs. Adams in the front pew.

If Mr. Adams were not living, Kate could choose a brother, uncle, godfather, or close family friend to escort her up the aisle. Mrs. Adams would say, "I do," from her place in the pew. She could step forward if she wished, but it is not necessary. If both parents were deceased, Kate's escort would say, "I do."

More and more often, brides who have been brought up in a one-parent home and who are very close to their mothers ask if she may escort them up the aisle. She may, if that is what will bring the most happiness to everyone involved.

BRIDESMAID — USHER

BRIDESMAID — USHER

MAID OF HONOR — BEST MAN

FLOWER GIRL — RING BEARER

BRIDE — GROOM

CHRISTIAN RECESSIONAL

If you are at all concerned about tradition, however, it is better to have a male escort.

It is also becoming more common for a bride to walk unescorted, if she prefers. There is no rule that says she must be escorted, only tradition which symbolically had the father or other male relative transfer or "give" the bride from his household to her groom's. Because this is no longer the way of the world as we know it, it is also more customary to have the minister either delete the "who gives . . ." section from the ceremony, or change it to, "Who will support this marriage?" or "Who will support this marriage with love and prayers?" to which everyone may respond, or to which the parents of both bride and groom may respond. At Beth's and Ben's wedding, their minister could even ask, "Who will support this new family?" or "Who will support this new family with their love and prayers" allowing Beth, Ben, and Ben's two children to answer together.

Some ministers signal the congregation to be seated as soon as the procession arrives at the front of the church. Others give the signal at this point in the ceremony, just before the principals move up to the altar. The pastor turns and walks to the altar, followed by Kate and Brian. The maid of honor and the best man accompany them, and the flower girl and ring bearer also follow, still in their relative positions. Kate hands her bouquet to her maid of honor, and the couple plight their troth. When it is time for the ring to be given, the best man takes it from the ring bearer's cushion (or from his pocket, if the ring bearer is carrying a facsimile) and hands it to the minister. The minister blesses it and gives it to Brian, who puts it on Kate's finger. Before going to the church, Kate had transferred her engagement ring to her right hand, since the wedding ring should never be put on outside the engagement ring. If Kate and Brian were having a double-ring ceremony, the maid of honor would then hand Brian's ring to the pastor, and the procedure would be repeated. In some churches, both rings are given to the pastor to be blessed at the same time.

The ceremony proceeds, with a blessing and a prayer, and at the end, the pastor pronounces Kate and Brian "husband and wife." Some clergymen are still saying "man and wife." If this is disagreeable to you, you may ask him to change it to "husband and wife." They kiss, and the organ plays the recessional. The maid of honor hands Kate her bouquet and straightens her train for her as she starts. The flower girl and ring bearer walk together behind the bride and the groom, followed by the maid of honor and the best man. The other attendants step forward two at a time and pair off, each usher escorting a bridesmaid down the aisle. When there are more ushers than bridesmaids, the extra men follow the couples, walking in pairs. If there is an odd man, he walks alone at the end. Kate could decide that she prefers the bridesmaids and ushers to walk out as they came in—bridesmaids together and ushers together—but Kate and Brian like the symbolism of their arriving separately, like the bride and groom, and leaving together after the marriage has taken place.

After the Ceremony

The photographer, who has remained at the back of the church after taking pictures of the bride's arrival, may now catch the radiant couple as they come down the aisle. He should never, in any circumstances, be allowed to follow the procession up to the chancel or take pictures during the ceremony. The flash and click of the shutter are distracting and greatly detract from the solemnity and beauty of the service.

The videographer, who had received permission from the pastor to video-tape quietly from the balcony, quickly moves to the back of the church and joins the photographer in catching the wedding party coming down the aisle.

The cars are waiting at the entrance. Kate and Brian are handed into the first one by the best man and leave for the reception. Whether they have a limousine with a chauffeur, or are driven in a borrowed car by the best man, the newlyweds sit in the back seat. As soon as the entire procession has reached the vestibule or entry, the ushers turn back to escort Kate's and Brian's close relatives out. Kate's mother and father enter the waiting limousine; Brian's mother is driven by her son, Michael. Others in the reserved pews walk out by themselves and as soon as they have left, the same two ushers who put the white ribbons in place remove them. The guests start to leave, and the ushers hurry on to the reception. The maid of honor and the bridesmaids, in the meantime, have entered the same limousines they arrived in and have left for the reception.

Beth and Ben, on the other hand, have decided to have their formal wedding pictures taken outside the church rather than at the reception, and they have more guests at the ceremony than will be at the reception. For these two reasons, they form their receiving line beginning in the vestibule and extending out the front doors. In this way, they are able to greet *all* their guests, and those who are going on to the reception may do so and be offered a drink and hors d'oeuvres while they wait for the wedding party to arrive.

The Minister's or Rabbi's Fee

The best man, if he has not already delivered the fee, does so before he leaves. The amount varies according to the size and formality of the ceremony. It may range from $50 for a small, private wedding to from $100 to $300 for an elaborate one. For Kate's and Brian's wedding, $200 is given in the form of a check made out to the pastor himself and enclosed in an envelope. If the minister prefers that the check be made out to the church instead, he will inform the groom of this choice.

When a minister or rabbi comes from a distance to perform the ceremony, travel and lodging expenses are paid for by the family at whose request the trip was made. Assuming that he has been asked because he is a close friend or relative of the bride or groom, it is likely that he will not accept a gift of money, in which case a thoughtful personal gift is most appropriate.

Receiving Line at the Church

If there is to be no reception, or if it is limited to family members, the bride and groom may stop and greet their guests at the back of the church, as did Ben and Beth. This is never done if most of those present are going on to the reception. The receiving line consists of the bride's mother, the groom's mother, the bride, the groom, and then the bridesmaids, if they are to be included. The fathers need not, but may, stand in line. If they do, they stand to the left of their wives.

Jewish Weddings

Jewish weddings generally take place on Saturday evening or on Sunday, since a marriage may not take place on the Sabbath—from sundown on Friday until sundown on Saturday. There are certain other times that are forbidden, such as Holy Days, a period during the summer, and during part of Passover. The bride and groom must choose the best time with the help of their rabbi. Since many other procedures are dictated by individual rabbis or by local custom rather than by canon law, it is essential that all the details be discussed with the rabbi who will perform the marriage.

Although some Jewish wedding are held in synagogues, they need not be; therefore many are held in hotels, halls, or clubs. Ceremony and reception are held in the same place. Often the bride and her family receive their guests before the ceremony in a room off the hall where the wedding will be held. This is also true when the wedding is held in a synagogue. In Orthodox or Conservative ceremonies, the bride's family is seated on the right side of the hall, the groom's on the left.

Jewish brides, whether Orthodox, Conservative, or Reform, wear conventional wedding dresses. The correct clothes for attendants are the same as those for a Christian ceremony, described earlier. At Conservative and Orthodox weddings, however, all the men, attendants as well as guests, must wear *yarmulkes* (skullcaps) or, if the wedding attire is formal, top hats, during the ceremony. They may be taken off after a Conservative wedding ceremony but must be worn during both ceremony and reception at Orthodox weddings.

Orthodox and Conservative ceremonies differ somewhat from Reform ser-

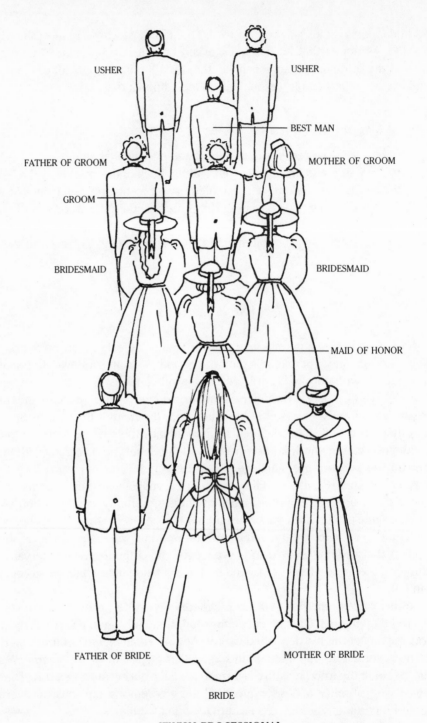

JEWISH PROCESSIONAL

| BRIDESMAIDS | FATHER OF BRIDE | MOTHER OF BRIDE | MAID OF HONOR | | BRIDE | GROOM | BEST MAN | | MOTHER OF GROOM | FATHER OF GROOM | USHERS |

RABBI

JEWISH CEREMONY, AT THE ALTAR

vices. In the Orthodox and Conservative services the processional is led by the ushers, followed by the bridesmaids. The rabbi comes next (accompanied by the cantor, if one is participating in the ceremony), then the best man, and next the groom, walking between his parents. The maid of honor follows them, and the bride, escorted by her parents, comes last. The Orthodox bride is always veiled. The ceremony is performed under a canopy called a *chuppah.* Formerly this chuppah was held over the heads of the bride and groom and their parents as they walked up the aisle. Today, however, it is already in place at the end of the hall; in a synagogue it is in front of the Ark. The chuppah is sometimes made of flowers, but it is generally a richly decorated cloth.

The bride and groom and the two honor attendants stand under the chuppah during the ceremony, and, if it is large enough, the parents may stand there also. The rabbi stands facing them beside a white-covered table containing two glasses of wine. The Orthodox service is read mostly in Hebrew, with certain parts in English or the couple's language. The rabbi first blesses the wine and gives the goblet to the groom, who sips and then gives it to his bride. A document is read in Aramaic, giving in detail the pledge of fidelity and protection on the part of

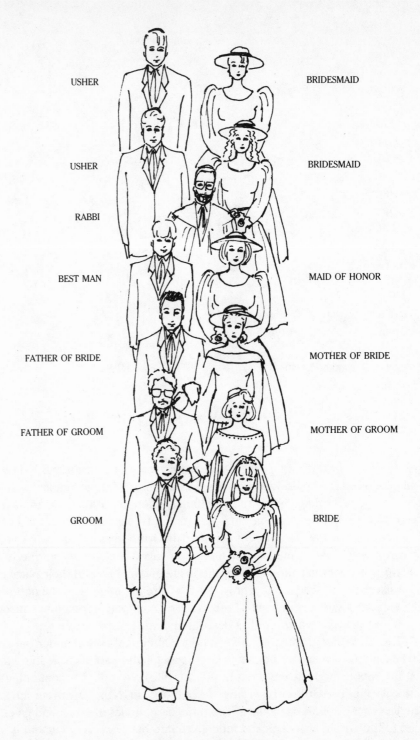

USHER

BRIDESMAID

USHER

BRIDESMAID

RABBI

BEST MAN

MAID OF HONOR

FATHER OF BRIDE

MOTHER OF BRIDE

FATHER OF GROOM

MOTHER OF GROOM

GROOM

BRIDE

JEWISH RECESSIONAL

the groom and indicating the bride's contribution to the new household. The groom places a plain gold ring on his bride's right index finger, which she may later move to the conventional fourth finger, left hand. The groom says, "Thou art consecrated unto me with this ring, according to the law of Moses and Israel." This is followed by an address by the rabbi to the congregation and the couple on the sanctity of marriage. Finally, the Seven Blessings are given, and the couple drinks from the second cup of wine. At the conclusion of the ceremony the wine goblet is broken by the groom to symbolize the destruction of the temple in Jerusalem, which serves as a reminder that one must never lose sight of the past, even on happy occasions.

The bride and groom always lead the recessional. The order of the bridal party may vary, but generally the two sets of parents follow, then the maid of honor with the best man, the rabbi (and cantor if there is one), and finally the bridesmaids and ushers.

The Reform service is usually very similar to a Christian wedding. English is used, and the canopy may be dispensed with. The groom is ushered in by his best man, and the bride is escorted by her father. The order of attendants is the same as in a Christian ceremony. The groom may repeat the responses in either Hebrew or English. The bride and groom do, as in the Orthodox ceremony, drink wine from the same cup, symbolizing the cup of joy. The bride's father, although he escorts her, does not give her away in a Jewish ceremony.

The reception following a Jewish wedding is similar to that described for a Christian marriage. A grace is always said over the feast.

Roman Catholic Ceremonies

Many Catholic weddings are centered around a nuptial mass, and traditionally these took place between eight and twelve in the morning. In many churches, a nuptial mass may now take place in the afternoon.

In marriage ceremonies that do not include participation in a mass, the service is quite similar to the Protestant ceremony. In this case the bridal couple go to their church and take Communion together earlier in the day.

Roman Catholic weddings may be held at any time of the year. The marriages are announced by banns, proclaimed from the pulpit three times, or they may be published in the church calendar prior to the wedding. Therefore, plans must be made at least that far in advance. This is a common practice for some Protestant denominations, as well.

The bride's father escorts her up the aisle but does not give her away. As soon as she has given her hand to the groom, the bride's father joins his wife in the front pew. Other details, such as whether or not the bridal party will stand within the altar rail, are determined by individual churches. The priest will discuss these practices when he talks to the couple and at the rehearsal.

While the Catholic Church prefers that both the best man and maid of honor be Catholics, at least one must be. The other attendants need not be Catholic, but they are instructed in how to genuflect, and other procedures, before the ceremony.

Catholics may serve as ushers and bridesmaids in a Protestant wedding.

When a nuptial mass follows the marriage ceremony, the bridal party is usually seated—in the choir stalls, perhaps, or sometimes the two front pews are reserved for them. The bride and groom are seated on two chairs before the altar. There is generally a kneeling bench. The maid of honor and the best man remain in the sanctuary with the bride and groom. Otherwise, the processional, the arrangements during the ceremony, the recessional, and most other details are like those described for a Protestant wedding.

When a non-Catholic marries a Catholic there are other regulations to be considered. Some are universal, others are imposed at the discretion of the officiating priest. In any case, they will be explained to the couple when they confer with the priest before the wedding and the young people must abide by the church's rules. Very often couples of different faiths have two ceremonies, that of one faith following immediately after the other. Another alternative is to have the clergy of each faith present to perform different parts of the ceremony.

Ceremonies of Other Religions

The three most widely practiced faiths in the United States, Protestant, Jewish, and Catholic, are covered in this book, but there may be occasions when the opportunity arises to attend the wedding of friends of other faiths or nationalities. I recently attended a wedding in a Greek Orthodox church where the bride and groom, with the help of their priest, had prepared a lovely program for each wedding guest which explained the order and the meaning of various traditions and practices that would take place during the ceremony. This helped make the ceremony more meaningful for those of us who had not attended a Greek Orthodox wedding before and allowed us to participate more fully.

Another time I attended a beautiful Egyptian garden wedding where the bride and the groom, dressed in lovely ornamental costume, were brought various bowls into which they placed their feet during the wedding ceremony. The service was conducted in both Arabic and English so those non-Arabic-speaking guests would be able to follow along and understand the symbolism of the bowls and the customs.

In both cases, although the actual ceremonies were different, according to their own religious beliefs, the treatment and seating of guests and the following receptions were very similar to those of Protestant, Catholic and Jewish weddings. These pages, therefore, may serve as a guide to brides and grooms of several faiths, enabling them to adjust areas where customs are different, and use as a reference those areas where there are similarities.

A guest invited to a wedding of a faith not covered in detail here should not hesitate to admit to not knowing all that may be required of a guest and asking if there is anything he or she should know in advance of attending the wedding. It is perfectly all right to call the host, or the bride or groom, whomever you are closer to, or to call a church, temple, or synagogue office and ask. Your enjoyment and experience will be all the richer when you feel confident that you have not overlooked something that may be expected of you.

For example, a guest attending a Jewish wedding for the first time may think he must buy a yarmulke in order to follow religious regulations and attend. It is reassuring to know that most synagogues have a box of yarmulkes outside the entrance to the temple, and yarmulkes are provided when the wedding takes place at a catering hall or club, as well, when they are required of male guests. It is expected that, out of respect, all male guests will wear a yarmulke when it is required, but it is not expected that they will go out and buy one so both thoughtfulness and religious requirements suggest that they be provided.

Non-Catholic guests are not expected to genuflect or to cross themselves during a Catholic ceremony, or to recite a creed or confess to a faith that is not their own. They are expected, however, to rise and be seated with everyone else, out of respect for the religion. This is true of any place of worship you enter as a wedding guest. When unsure, simply follow the lead of other guests.

9

THE RECEPTION

It is important that the ushers do not escort the families out of the church and remove the ribbons from the pews too quickly. They must not wait so long that the guests become restless, but a slight delay allows the bride, the groom, and the bridesmaids to get to the place where the reception will be held before the crowd arrives. It also lessens the wait of the guests while formal pictures of the bridal party are being taken.

In planning the location of the receiving line, the bride's mother should, if possible, see that there is considerable space where the guests form the line. Sometimes the crowd arriving from the church is packed into a small hallway or, in some cases, cannot even get into the building, and this is most uncomfortable for everyone. While the area to which they will pass after greeting the bride is of primary importance, the waiting area is important too, especially if the photography takes longer than expected. One solution is to have a few tables and chairs set up in the room where the line forms. Refreshments are served to the guests as they arrive and, as the line lengthens, an usher near the door suggests that later arrivals take a seat until the line is shorter, thus avoiding a very long wait.

Photographs

When the bridal party is all assembled at the place where the reception is held, the formal pictures of the wedding party are taken. This can be somewhat of an inconvenience to the guests who are waiting to go through the receiving line, but there is no other possible time. If they wait until the line is broken up, the women's attire and hairdos may be less fresh and neat, and the bride and groom and their parents may be beginning to show the strain. The only remedy is to get everyone together quickly and ask the photographer to take as little time as possible.

The Receiving Line

If the bride and groom have not decided to have their receiving line directly after the ceremony and form the line, instead, after picture taking and at the site of the reception, they form it, as mentioned before, in a location which permits guests to have refreshments while they are waiting their turn and which leads them to the more open area where the reception will take place. Guests should not go through the receiving line either eating or drinking. They should put down their glasses and plates beforehand.

Kate and Brian form their receiving line at the club. Kate's mother stands first in the line, to greet the guests. Her father is next, followed by Mrs. Jamison. It is not required that fathers stand in the receiving line. Some prefer to circulate among the guests during this time, instead, but many are happy to stand in the line to be sure to have a chance to greet and meet everyone—something they might not otherwise be able to do, particularly at a very large reception. Were Mr. Jamison living, he would stand in the line, too, directly after his wife. It is a general guideline that when one father is part of the receiving line, the other should be, too.

Divorced parents should not stand in the line together. Even if not embarrassing to them, it would surely be confusing to some of the guests. The parent and stepparent with whom the bride or groom has spent the most time, or the ones who are giving the wedding, are the ones who should be in the line. If neither has remarried and both are helping give the reception, it is far easier to go by the rule of thumb that fathers needn't stand in the line and have only the bride's mother there. In the rare circumstance when divorced parents are especially friendly and accept one another's new spouses, and when both couples are giving the wedding, they may all stand in the receiving line, but the couples should be separated by the groom's parents to avoid creating too much confusion.

Kate is positioned next to her new mother-in-law, with Brian to her left. The maid of honor stands beside Brian. Kate has excused her bridesmaids from the receiving line, as she feels it is difficult for both them and the guests to prolong

MOTHER OF BRIDE   MOTHER OF GROOM   BRIDE   GROOM   MAID OF HONOR BRIDESMAID BRIDESMAID

FATHER OF BRIDE   FATHER OF GROOM
(OPTIONAL)   (OPTIONAL)

RECEIVING LINE

unnecessarily the polite remarks one must make. If she wished to have them with her, however, it would be quite correct. Young children—flower girls, ring bearers, pages and train bearers—never stand in the line.

Handicapped parents or parents in ill health may take their place in the line seated on a high stool, if that is possible, or otherwise in a solid chair or their wheelchair.

The guests pass by as quickly as possible, pausing only long enough to be greeted by their hostess, to wish Kate happiness, and to congratulate the groom. Close friends usually accompany their handshake with a kiss. Otherwise, each person extends a hand to the person in line, who turns to introduce him or her to the next person in line before greeting the next guest. This eliminates the guest from having to introduce him- or herself to every person in the line and makes the process more personal. No one should delay the line with extended conversation. If Kate remembers a wedding gift received from the person she is greeting, she should mention it and how much she appreciated it, but that is all. She should then pass the guest along to Brian to greet.

There is some feeling against having a receiving line at all, but it does serve an important purpose, especially at a very large wedding where the groom is a stranger to many of the guests. The line is the only way in which every guest can meet the groom and/or his parents and offer congratulations. It would be almost impossible for the newlyweds to speak to everyone just by circulating among the tables, which makes the receiving invaluable and irreplaceable.

At a very formal wedding there is occasionally an announcer standing directly before the bride's mother. This is especially helpful if she does not know a number of the guests on the groom's side. The announcer asks the guests for their names as they approach and repeats the names to the mother of the bride.

David's and Susan's wedding, because it is small and intimate, does not require a receiving line and they have chosen to eliminate it, feeling that they will be able to speak, at least briefly, to all their guests during the reception.

Ben and Beth have gone against the guideline that children do not stand in the receiving line and included Ben's young son and daughter to allow them to be a part of receiving the good wishes of the guests and to feel a sense of participation with their father and new stepmother.

Just beyond the end of Brian's and Kate's receiving line there is a waiter standing with a tray of glasses filled with champagne to offer to guests as they pass on their way into the room where the rest of the reception is taking place.

The Guest Book

It is not obligatory, but some couples like to have their friends sign a guest register to have as a memento of the occasion. If so, the book is placed on a table near the entrance or at the end of the receiving line. A member of the family, a friend, or one of the bridesmaids or junior bridesmaids stays beside it to remind each guest (or one member of each couple) to sign. Very rarely, a guest book is placed instead at the entrance to the ceremony and one of the ushers asks guests to sign it before entering the sanctuary. This is done particularly when more guests are attending the ceremony than will be attending the reception. If the guest book is signed at the church or synagogue, another is not placed at the reception.

The Bride's Table

Kate and Brian decided they would like to be seated with their attendants, and a long table is set up for them at one side of the room. After every guest has been greeted in the receiving line, the couple leads the way to the table. They sit at the center of the long side that faces the room so that the guests may see them. The maid of honor sits on Brian's left, and the best man on Kate's right. The other attendants sit on either side, and their wives or husbands are also seated at the table. Insofar as possible, men and women alternate. Kate has planned a congenial seating arrangement, and earlier in the day her mother went to the club and distributed place cards.

Whether the food is served buffet style to the guests or not, the bridal table is always served by the waiters as any sit-down meal would be. If Kate and Brian had had fewer attendants, their closest friends could have been asked to join them at the bridal table.

When There Is No Bride's Table

Many couples prefer to circulate among their guests rather than to be seated at a bridal table. This is perfectly correct and lends an atmosphere of informality even to a very large wedding. There should, however, be one table reserved—large enough to seat all the attendants—so that the bride and groom may always have a place to sit down. Not only are they apt to be tired after standing in the receiving line or dancing with a great many guests, but they should be assured of a place where they can be seated to eat.

When there is no bride's table, the bride and groom go to the buffet table themselves and take their plates to the table reserved for them. The waiters may offer to serve their plates and carry the food for them, in which case they accept graciously and go directly to their seats.

The table need not be specially decorated, but there should be a bridal centerpiece or a "reserved" card on it, so that other people will not seat themselves there. As at a bridal table, the bouquets of the bridesmaids and the bride are placed on the table, complementing the centerpiece. Either type of table should be large enough to accommodate the bouquets, since the bridal party cannot be expected to continue to carry them and has nowhere else to put them during the reception. The cake is not placed on this table but on a separate table with wheels so that it may be rolled to the center of the room for the cutting ceremony.

The bridesmaids and ushers do not necessarily all seat themselves at the same time if they are enjoying the dancing or talking to friends. The best man must, however, get them all together shortly after the receiving line breaks up in order that they may join him in toasting the newlyweds. He may do this at the reserved table, or he may simply ask them all to come to the middle of the room or some other convenient place.

The attendants also gather around when the bride and groom are about to cut the cake. Otherwise, when there is no bridal table, they mingle with the guests, coming back to the couple frequently to see if there is anything they can do for them.

The Parents' Table

Ideally, those seated at the parents' table are the mother and father of both bride and groom, the grandparents, the minister or rabbi who performs the ceremony and his or her spouse, and, if possible, the godparents. Mrs. Jamison is seated to the right of Mr. Adams, the pastor is seated to Mrs. Adams' left, and the others at the table in whatever order Mrs. Adams thinks best. Were Mr. Jamison to be living, he would be seated on Mrs. Adams' right. This table is usually set close to the bridal table, a little apart from the tables for the other guests. In some cases, the number of special guests far exceeds the number of places available at the table. This is particularly true when there are four sets of grandparents, for example. In this instance, the bride's parents would host one table and the groom's parents a second, each adding additional relatives or close friends, as space permitted. The minister or rabbi and his or her spouse would

PARENTS' TABLE

usually be seated at the bride's parents table, unless he or she had been invited by the groom's parents in which case he or she would be seated with them. I feel strongly that whenever possible, there should be only one parents' table, in the true spirit of "joining" that a wedding should have.

If the parents of either bride or groom are divorced, they would not be seated at the same table. A separate table would be arranged for the parent less closely connected with the wedding and his or her special guests.

Place Cards

When there is to be a seated dinner there are always place cards for the bridal table and the parents' table or tables, and frequently place cards for guest tables, as well. Rather than expect guests to wander from table to table looking for their assigned seat, tables are often numbered and the place cards numbered accordingly and arranged, in alphabetical order, on a side table at the entrance to the reception. After leaving the receiving line, guests pass by the table and find their place card. They then look at the number written on the card and enter the reception area to locate the table with the same number.

Kate and her mother, at their final meeting with the club manager, had received a diagram of the number of tables and their placement from him which they used to prepare their seating plan and number each place card.

When guests are to be seated at a particular table, I highly recommend that the tables not be divided down the middle of the room with guests of the bride's family on one side and guests of the groom's family on the other. This is particularly unfriendly and I much prefer that they be interspersed throughout the room. Whereas this is not the time to mix and match and guests have a much better time when seated with people they know, I do feel that the tables themselves should be mixed, with a group of the bride's friends and family next to a group of the groom's friends and family, and so on.

If there are no place cards for guest tables, then guests form their own groups or find places with a group already seated, saying, "May we join you?"

Tables for Guests

Obviously, if a full meal is to be served, there must be seating for all guests. But even at a cocktail reception, there should be enough tables and chairs so that guests can find a place to sit down and enjoy their appetizers, drinks and wedding cake. If a meal is to be served, tables are formally set with a cloth (usually white but sometimes in the same color family as the bridesmaids' dresses), a centerpiece of flowers, and complete place settings.

At less formal buffet or cocktail receptions, tables are covered with a cloth but there may or may not be centerpieces. Usually flatware is set at the tables for a buffet reception, but it sometimes is with the plates on the buffet.

A Master of Ceremonies

A most unfortunate custom that has arisen in recent years is the hiring of a master of ceremonies for weddings. This individual runs the reception like a stage presentation, telling principals and guests what to do and announcing each event like a circus ringmaster. The bridal party, the parents of the bride and groom, and the bride and groom themselves are made to enter the room one at a time, after guests are seated, their names shouted over a microphone, for the guests to applaud. This master of ceremonies usually tells jokes, and intrudes his comments about all aspects of the event as they occur. I was at one wedding where a master of ceremonies, when the lights had been dimmed and cherries jubilee rolled in, alight and dramatic, actually shouted, "Let's hear it for the flaming cherries!" All the charm and intimacy of a private affair, which a wedding certainly should be, is completely lost. For many, many years no one ever thought of having a master of ceremonies, and there is no need for one now. Commercial catering and bridal services have promoted the idea, but it is in very poor taste.

Toasts at the Reception

As mentioned before, the guests may be served champagne before and after they pass through the receiving line. If it is a very formal wedding, however, where everyone will be seated at tables set for a full meal, the guests go immediately to find their places and the champagne is served to them there.

At the bridal table, the bride's glass is filled first, the groom's next, and then those of the attendants, starting with the maid of honor. As soon as all the glasses are filled and the guests have been served, the best man rises and makes the first toast to the couple. These toasts are usually short and rather sentimental. At a very large wedding, it is often necessary for the best man to go to the microphone used by the band or orchestra so that he can be heard. Other members of the bridal party may propose toasts, and the groom invariably toasts his bride and his new parents-in-law.

Everyone rises for the toast to the bride and the groom except the bride and groom, who remain seated. If a toast is directed to the bride only, the groom rises, and if it is directed to their parents, they both rise.

If there is no bridal table, the attendants form a group when the receiving line breaks up, and the best man, asking for silence, offers his toast.

Reading Congratulatory Messages

When telegrams have been received from friends and relatives who cannot be at the wedding, they are usually read aloud following the toasts. Tom Coleman, Brian's best man, does this and then gives the telegrams to Kate's parents so that the bride and groom will be able to enjoy and acknowledge them at another time.

Dancing at the Reception

When a full meal is served and there will be special dances beginning with the bride and the groom, followed by the bride and her father-in-law, the bride and her father, and so forth, the dancing does not begin until after dessert is finished. When the only special dance is the one of the bride and groom, after which their attendants join them and encourage other guests to dance, too, the dancing may begin immediately after the toasts are made so that guests, who may not dance until the bride and groom have led the way, may dance between courses. Although this practice has been frowned upon in the past, a full meal can take up to an hour and one-half to be served, course by course, and it is pleasant for all guests to be able to combine table conversation with dancing during this time.

At a less formal, buffet-style reception, dancing usually begins as soon as the bride and groom have had a chance to rest their feet after standing in the receiving line.

Kate and Brian decide they would like to have ordered dancing at their reception. They dance the first dance together, having previously told the orchestra leader the song they want played. Ordinarily, the groom's father would ask the bride for the second dance, but in this case, Kate dances next with her father and Brian with Kate's mother. The best man cuts in on Kate's father, who then asks Brian's mother to dance. Were the groom to have a father, he would dance at this time with the bride's mother, after which the dancing becomes general. Each usher should dance with the bride and all the bridesmaids. It is usual for as many men as possible to cut in on the bride.

Music may be provided by anything from a single accordion to a ten-piece band. As mentioned earlier, most elaborate receptions sometimes have two orchestras, to ensure continuous music. At very simple parties, a tape player solves the problem of music economically and beautifully.

The Menu

The food is chosen according to the time of day and the formality of the wedding. When a reception immediately follows a formal early-morning wedding, the menu is similar to that for a brunch or elaborate breakfast. The menu after a formal late-morning wedding is simply a typical luncheon menu.

After an informal afternoon wedding, the food is served as a buffet. A "tea" menu consisting of sandwiches and cake is offered. If it is semiformal rather than informal, cocktail buffet food is offered, adding hot hors d'oeuvres such as small quiches, miniature pizza, chicken or beef saté with a peanut sauce, and Greek spinach and feta cheese triangles in phyllo pastry.

The formal late-afternoon reception offers a full supper or dinner. In winter the menu consists of a clear soup, a fish course, a main course of chicken or meat and a hot vegetable, and dessert. In summer the food may be cold—jellied madrilèene, cold poached salmon, salad, and dessert—but in either case it provides a complete meal.

Specific menu suggestions will be found in chapter 14.

Cutting the Wedding Cake

The bride's cake is used for this ceremony, which is one of the highlights of the reception. At a sit-down reception the cake is cut just before dessert is served, and slices are served with the ices or ice cream. When the reception is a buffet, the cake is cut later, usually shortly before the bride and groom leave.

Kate cuts the first two slices, with Brian helping her by placing his hand over hers. He feeds her the first bite and she feeds him the second. When this ceremony is completed, a waiter cuts the rest of the cake, and others pass it to the guests. Sometimes the small top layer is made of fruitcake, which can be preserved by freezing, and many couples do freeze this top layer. The idea is that on each anniversary they will have a small piece of their original wedding cake to enjoy. When the cake is topped with an ornament, this too is naturally kept for the couple.

The End of the Reception

It is a great mistake to prolong the reception unnecessarily. Even though the bride and groom and their guests are thoroughly enjoying the party, the wise couple will leave before becoming too exhausted. If the cake were cut and served as dessert, Kate and Brian would leave sometime later, after dancing and chatting with all their friends, or in time to make a plane or boat. But since their reception is buffet-style, the cake-cutting ceremony takes place later and is the signal that they are about to depart. After the cake has been cut, Kate signals her bridesmaids, and they gather at the foot of the stairs as she goes to change her clothes. If there were no stairs, they would stand in a doorway or near any spot where she might conveniently stop to throw her bouquet. To show no favoritism, Kate turns her back and tosses the bouquet over her shoulder. As the bridesmaid who catches the bouquet is supposed to be the next to get married, if Kate knows there is one planning to follow soon in her footsteps, she might unobtrusively aim the flowers in that direction.

In some communities the bride wears her ornamental blue garter just below her knee so that the groom can remove it easily and throw it to his ushers. The one who catches it will be the next to marry.

Mrs. Adams and the bridesmaids accompany Kate to the dressing room and stay with her while she changes into her going-away clothes. Brian goes to the room reserved for him with his best man, who helps him change and packs up the wedding outfit. As soon as both bride and groom are ready, they meet at the top of the stairs and say good-bye to their ushers and bridesmaids. Before she leaves the dressing room, Kate thoughtfully sends a bridesmaid to ask her father and new in-laws to come and say good-bye to her.

The attendants hurry down to get their supply of paper rose petals—infinitely prettier and easier to clean up than rice—and see that all the guests have theirs. The best man leads the way down the stairs and through the crowd to the waiting car. The guests pelt Kate and Brian with the petals as they pass, calling good-bye and best wishes. Bride and groom jump into the car and drive off, leaving their friends and relatives to have a final drink or dance and to discuss every detail of the lovely wedding.

Belated Receptions

Occasionally a reception must be held a week or two after the ceremony takes place. This may happen when a member of the armed forces gets married where he is stationed and the couple returns home a little later, or in other similar circumstances. The bride's family, whether they attended the wedding or not, may wish to give the couple a reception. If there was no formal reception following the wedding ceremony, the one given later may be exactly as it would have been had it been held the day of the wedding. The bride may wear her wedding dress if she wishes, in order to show it to all the friends and relatives who could not attend the ceremony. There should be a wedding cake and all the other accompaniments of a reception that the bride and groom would like to include. Invitations may be engraved or they may be on the bride's parents' notepaper, with "In honor of Ensign and Mrs. Cogswell" written on the top.

A Reception in the Parish House

A reception held in a parish house or the social rooms of a church or synagogue may offer a solution to the bride-to-be who lives by herself in a small room or apartment, or to a couple who cannot afford elaborate facilities and liquor. It is especially appropriate when a bride or her family has been closely connected with their church.

Many large churches and synagogues provide all the accessories—tablecloths, silver, china—and their staffs may even cater a buffet. In other churches the sandwiches and cake are prepared by relatives, friends, or an outside caterer. Fruit punch and soft drinks only are offered in most churches, although alcoholic beverages may be served in a synagogue. The bride and her family do as much decorating as they wish. Most parish halls have a record player; the records, if they are not available at the church, may be rented. If the church has a lawn or a garden, the doors may be opened so that guests may stand outside if the weather permits.

Family and friends who could not otherwise be asked to attend the wedding can come, and some may take part by assisting with pouring, serving, or registering guests. The expenses of hiring a hall, serving liquor, and having expensive catering help are avoided. The church, of course, must charge a nominal fee for food and services rendered, but it is small compared to the cost of using the facilities of a hall. Most important, the warmth and intimacy of the familiar religious surroundings lend an atmosphere of happiness often not achieved at far more elaborate receptions.

The Restaurant Reception

A small reception—usually a sit-down luncheon or dinner—is sometimes held in a restaurant. This is often done when the ceremony takes place before a justice of the peace or in a rectory. The family and friends of the couple, and the witnesses or attendants, make up the entire party.

If possible, the bride should choose a restaurant that can provide a private room. Otherwise the party may be the object of curiosity and comment from other diners, and the feeling of intimacy will be lost.

Some restaurants, especially those connected with a hotel, have very elaborate facilities, providing the wedding cake, photographer, live music for dancing, and decorations. You may, of course, use as many or as few of their facilities as you wish. Others provide only the food and service, and it is up to you to arrange for the additional items.

The dinner is usually ordered ahead of time, rather than having each guest consult the menu. There should be a wedding cake, no matter how simple, and the usual toasts are given by the best man and the groom. Otherwise, the reception is much like any other dinner party, and unless the restaurant has dance music, the guests and the bridal couple leave when the meal is over.

After-Reception Entertaining

When many out-of-town relatives and friends have come some distance for the wedding, the bride's mother often feels that she would like to have them in her home after the reception to have a chance to visit with them and so that they may see the gifts. If a full meal has not been served at the reception, she may even offer them dinner. This is a most generous thought, but it is a considerable amount of work in addition to all the wedding preparations. I can only recommend that anyone wishing to give such a party restrict the guest list to out-of-towners and immediate family. Otherwise she may find she is giving what amounts to a second reception.

A more practical solution, if it can be arranged, is to ask those particular guests to stop by to see the gifts, and then ask relatives or close friends to organize small groups to go out to dinner.

Party in Honor of a Bride and Groom

When a man marries a woman from a distant section of the country, often his friends and relatives are unable to take the time or spend the money to attend the wedding. However, after the honeymoon the couple may return to the groom's hometown to live, or at least for a visit. This is a good opportunity for his parents to invite family friends to a party in honor of the newlyweds. Apart from being a nice welcoming gesture to the bride, this provides a pleasant way for her to meet her in-laws' friends and relatives. It also allows the groom's family to have wedding announcements, rather than invitations, sent to those who could not possibly go to the wedding, since an invitation to this second party takes the place of an invitation to the original reception. Announcements relieve friends of the obligation of giving a gift, unless, of course, they wish to, even though they were not invited to the wedding.

The event may be as simple or as elaborate as their inclination and finances allow. However, it should not be an attempt to compete with the actual wedding reception. The invitations should not be sent in the same envelopes with the wedding invitations or announcements, if these are issued in the name of the bride's family. There should not be a wedding cake, nor should the members of the wedding party dress in their wedding clothes, with the exception of the bride, who may want those who did not attend the wedding to see her dress. After greeting all the arrivals, she may change into a cocktail dress to be more comfortable. The groom's parents may limit the affair to a tea or cocktail party given for an hour or two in the late afternoon, or they may have a complete buffet or sit-down dinner in the evening. It may be held at home or in a restaurant or at a club. Possibly a cocktail buffet provides the best solution.

Invitations should be sent out approximately two weeks in advance and they are often written on notepaper. Across the top of the note the groom's mother writes the words "In honor of Deirdre and Tom" and includes the date, the hour, and the address. If the party is to be quite formal, she may order engraved invitations or purchase engraved "fill-in" invitations, which leave spaces to write in the pertinent information. The fully engraved invitation would include "to meet (or, IN HONOR OF) Mr. and Mrs. Thomas Braden," in the wording.

The menu may vary a great deal. It can include a platter of iced seafood such as clams and oysters on the shell and shrimp with lemons, black pepper and cocktail sauce, ham baked in a crust with chutney butter, or veal Marengo (stewed with tomatoes and mushrooms). These main dishes can be served with gratin of potatoes, assorted breads, green salad with arugula or watercress and a zesty dressing, chocolate mousse, white and rosé wines, coffee and tea. Other buffet dishes that should be served from a chafing dish are beef chili, curry of lamb, shrimp, or chicken, and stir-fried vegetables.

The table should be covered with a white or pastel tablecloth; if there is room, a centerpiece of flowers or fruit is attractive, but the "bridey" type of decoration seen at a wedding reception should be avoided.

Although there is no formal receiving line, the bride and groom and his parents stay near the door to greet the arriving guests. Either the groom himself or one of his parents should introduce the bride to everyone she does not know.

If liquor is served, a bar should be set up in a convenient spot, one that will allow people to keep moving and will not block the hall or entrance to the main room. Arriving guests are expected to ask whoever is bartending for the drinks they want. If punch is offered, either with or without alcohol, the punchbowl may be set up in the same location described for a bar. There should always be a variety of soft drinks, tomato juice, colas, ginger ale, and tonic to be used as mixes and for those who prefer not to drink alcohol.

Music, especially if there is room to dance, adds to any party. If one's budget does not permit hiring an orchestra, a strolling accordion player will lend a festive air, and even records make a nice background. Any pictures of the wedding should be on display, or at least available to show the guests.

10

WEDDINGS IN SPECIAL SITUATIONS

When a couple decides not to have a traditional church or synagogue ceremony, they then consider other settings, such as a wedding at home, at the
site of the reception, such as a club, hotel or catering facility, and at a justice of
the peace. Other special wedding situations include weddings at an uncommon
time of day, and a military wedding, which is unique in the number of additional
people it involves.

The Wedding at Home

A wedding held at home requires more work for the bride's family, but it
often has an air of intimacy and a type of beauty that cannot be achieved in any
other setting. Whatever the size of the guest list, the house wedding can and
should be as perfect in every detail as the most elaborate church or synagogue
wedding.

Unless you live in a mansion or have spacious grounds, your guest list for
a wedding at home will be somewhat limited. Since it will most likely take place
in the largest room in the house, the list must be restricted to the number of
guests who can comfortably stand or preferably be seated in that room. Of course
if you live in an area where it can be guaranteed not to rain, or you wish to take
a very great chance, you may plan to have the wedding outside and invite as
many guests as your garden or lawn will hold.

The Ceremony

The ceremony itself is exactly the same as it is in a church or synagogue. An aisle leading from the entrance of the room to the space where the marriage will take place may be bordered by white satin ribbons suspended from stanchions. There may or may not be bouquets of flowers on each post. If the room is very large, chairs may be placed in rows for guests, but generally guests stand on either side of the aisle.

If it is required that the bridal couple kneel during a part of the ceremony, a cushioned bench is provided for the bride's and groom's use during the blessing. It is placed in front of the space where the minister or rabbi stands facing the guests and is usually backed by an altar rail. The ends of the rail, or the uprights at either end of the kneeling bench, are decorated with greens or sprays of flowers.

Your mother greets people as they arrive, or, if the wedding is formal, a maid usually opens the door for the guests and directs them to the room where they leave their coats, in cool weather, or to the room where the ceremony takes place and where your mother is standing at the entrance to welcome them. Your groom's mother and father take their places with the other guests, standing or seated in the front row on the right side of the aisle. If there are ushers, they are purely ornamental, as they do not escort guests to their places. Each arrival simply finds a spot from which to see as well as possible. The minister, on arrival, must be directed to a room in which to put on his or her vestments. Just before you begin walking up the aisle, your mother takes her place in the left front row. Guests who arrive late should be asked to remain in the hall until the ceremony is over.

Music is most often provided by a single musician or a small chamber music group, although a record or tape player may be used. The procession usually starts at the head of the stairs, or from the hallway outside the room for the ceremony.

The order of the processional is exactly like that in a church wedding, although there are rarely many attendants at a house wedding—two bridesmaids and two ushers are average, and four maximum, unless your house is immense. If the aisle is short, the ushers do not walk in the procession but take their places by the improvised altar when the music starts.

The minister or rabbi, the groom and the best man enter from another door and take their places as the music sounds. If the room has no other convenient entrance, they go up the aisle just before the procession starts.

In a home wedding, you and your groom never take a step together. He meets you at the place where the service is read, and there is no recessional. After congratulating you, the minister or rabbi steps aside, an usher removes the prayer bench, and your family and friends flock forward to offer their best wishes. If your house is large enough to hold the reception in another room, you and your attendants may move there to greet your friends.

The Decorations

The area where the ceremony takes place may be backed by a veritable bank of greenery or flowers, or a deep green velvet drapery may be hung against the wall, with no flowers except those on the altar rail. The white of the bride's dress and the pastels of the bridesmaids' stand out beautifully against such a simple background.

An altar rail can be rented from a florist or made by anyone in your family in the simplest fashion, as it can be covered by a drapery, greens, or flowers.

A wedding held in the garden can be decorated with an arch covered in flowers in front of which the minister, bride and groom stand, with an aisle created in the center of rows of chairs.

Flowers provide the only other decorations—additional large pots of flowers or flowering trees for an outside wedding (which can be rented from a major florist), flowers on the tops of stanchions inside, and a centerpiece for the bridal or buffet table. Other bouquets may be placed on a mantel, tables, newel posts, or wherever you and your mother think they look best. The flowers may, but need not, be all white; they may include pastel shades related to the color of the bridesmaids' dresses or they may blend with the decor of the rooms.

For more details concerning decorating, see Chapter 13.

After the Ceremony

There is sometimes a table for the bridal party set up in another room, but if space is limited, there usually are not tables for families and guests. Tables for the bridal party, parents, family and friends may be set up in the garden as long as you rent a marquee or tent in case of bad weather, depending on the type of refreshments served. At a simple reception of hors d'oeuvres, beverages and wedding cake, a few chairs and tables should be available, but seating is not generally set up for every guest as for a more formal meal, unless space permits. When a tent is used or when there is very large room inside permitting several tables, the flowery, garden theme can be carried out by the use of flowered tablecloths, hanging pots of cascading flowers, and so on. One wedding I attended in a tent in the back yard of the bride's parents was beautifully decorated with flowered sheets used as table cloths and napkins and buffet cloths in solid colors picked up from the floral print.

All the guests at a house wedding stay on to enjoy refreshments and drink

GARDEN WEDDING AT HOME

a toast to the bride and groom. You may offer nothing but punch and wedding cake served from a small table covered with a tea cloth. Or you may serve a complete meal, including a hot dish, salads, sandwiches, ices, cake, and champagne as well as punch or other drinks. If only your immediate family and a few friends are present, the entire group may be seated together at a lunch or dinner table.

The Bride's Costume

The bride may choose between a long white wedding gown (without a train) and a simple afternoon dress with flowers in her hair. Either is correct, but you must take into consideration the size of the wedding and the elaborateness of the other preparations. If you intend to have bridesmaids and ushers and a bridal table, for example, you will surely want to wear a traditional long gown.

When a Relative's or Friend's Home is Used

When space is limited in your home, a kind friend or relative may offer his or her house for the wedding. There is no difference in procedure from that of a wedding in your own home. The invitations are sent in your parents' name, and while the address for the ceremony is that of your friend, the address under the R.s.v.p. is yours or your parents'.

You or your family pay all the expenses and, of course, generously tip any servants in your friend's home who may have taken part. You should show your appreciation by most sincere thanks, accompanied by the loveliest gift you can find.

Evening Weddings

In the South, because of the daytime heat, and in many areas of the West, evening weddings are popular. They are generally held at eight or nine o'clock, with the reception immediately following.

Evening weddings are usually formal or at least semiformal, and the gowns of the bride and her attendants are the same as those for a formal daytime wedding. The groom, the best man, the ushers, and the fathers usually wear white tie, although a tuxedo is acceptable. Guests at the formal ceremony wear evening clothes. The women wear long dinner dresses (or short, if that is the current style), and the men wear dinner jackets—black or navy in winter, white in summer. The mothers of the couple usually wear long dresses. In small communities, or when it is known that it is to be a simple wedding, guests may wear what they would to a daytime wedding—cocktail dresses and business suits.

Because of the lateness of the hour, a meal is rarely served after an evening wedding. Refreshments generally consist of delicate sandwiches, cake, and champagne or punch. Coffee is often served, especially at an informal reception.

Morning Weddings

A formal Catholic wedding held in the morning is exactly like a ceremony held later in the day. The wedding breakfast may be held right afterward, with the refreshments those of an elaborate breakfast; or it may be held as a luncheon or a reception in the late afternoon or evening. The only difficulty with the afternoon or evening reception is that out-of-town guests and relatives must be entertained and taken care of during the hours between the ceremony and the reception. If you do not have enough family or kind friends to do this, the guests are at a loss as to where to go and what to do for most of the day.

Sometimes a couple wishes to get married informally in the morning, possibly because of the time allotted for their honeymoon or travel schedule. The bride wears a simple street dress or suit—the same one in which she will leave for her honeymoon. She usually wears a corsage, but if she prefers, she may carry a small bouquet or merely a prayer book. She usually has only one attendant, who chooses a pretty dress in a color that complements the bride's outfit. The groom and his best man wear business suits. Breakfast is served after the ceremony at the bride's home, or possibly in a restaurant. The menu is one for brunch—bowls of fruit, smoked trout or sausages with scrambled eggs, croissant, Danish pastries, coffee, wine. A round of champagne is passed to toast the bride and groom.

A Wedding at the Rectory

Those who do not wish to have a church wedding and cannot have one at home may be married by their clergyman in the rectory. Only members of the family and a few close friends attend. The bride and groom arrive together, and when they see that all the guests are present the ceremony takes place. The only attendants are a maid of honor and a best man. The bride may wear a simple white gown if she wishes, but usually she chooses a becoming afternoon or cocktail dress. She may carry a bouquet if she wishes.

There may be no reception at all, in which case the guests offer their congratulations and depart. However, there may be a celebration at the bride's home, at the home of a friend, in the parish house, or in a hotel or restaurant. The reception may include many more friends than those invited to the ceremony.

Marriage Before a Justice of the Peace

Except that the bride never wears a wedding gown this wedding is very much like that in a rectory. There must be two witnesses present, so if the couple has no friends attending, the justice of the peace asks staff or family members to serve.

The ceremony is attended by only a few close relatives and friends in any case, and the group may or may not, according to the couple's wishes, go on to a meal or small celebration in a restaurant or at home.

Elopements

To most of us, an elopement means that a couple has married without consent of the parents. However, I suspect that many such marriages are known to the families and take place with their blessing.

When the bride's parents have already approved it, or accept it gracefully after the wedding takes place, they send out announcements in their name. But if they are unalterably opposed to the marriage, the newlyweds, instead, send them in their own names. The announcements may be sent even after some months have elapsed, and they include the location of the marriage and the date.

The bride's mother and father often give a belated reception (see page 166) when they are told of the marriage, generally a rather informal affair attended by relatives and close friends. Often this is done to introduce a groom who comes from another town. The invitations, written on notepaper, read, "In honor of Mr. and Mrs. John Baker" (the bride and groom), or "In honor of Sue and John."

The Military Wedding

The outstanding feature of a military wedding—and the only one that differs from those of other ceremonies—is the arch of swords through which the bride and groom pass at the end of the ceremony. Only commissioned officers are allowed this honor. As soon as the service is over, the ushers (if they are also officers) line up at the foot of the chancel steps. At the head usher's command, "Draw swords," they hold up their swords (blades up) in such a way as to form an arch. The couple passes through, the head usher says, "Return swords," and the men put them back in their sheaths. They then turn and escort the bridesmaids down the aisle.

Alternatively, the arch may be formed outside the church entrance. The ushers leave by a side door, hurry to the front of the church, and are waiting, swords raised, when the couple emerges. The bridesmaids walk out two by two but do not pass through the arch.

Any civilian ushers in the party line up beside the others and merely stand at attention as the bride and groom pass by. Therefore, unless the ushers are all officers, it is wiser to omit this ceremony since the effect would otherwise be somewhat ragged.

More information about the wearing of uniforms can be found in chapter 6.

The Double Wedding

Double weddings almost always involve two sisters, although occasionally cousins, close friends, or even two brothers wish to be married at the same time. To present the picture most clearly, let us say that Cindy is marrying Steve, and her younger sister, Linda, is marrying Mike. The procession is formed in this way: Both grooms' ushers go first, with Steve's attendants leading. Cindy's bridesmaids come next, then her maid of honor and then Cindy, the older sister, with her father. Linda's bridesmaids follow, then her maid of honor, and Linda comes last, walking with an older brother, or her nearest male relative, or close family friend.

The two grooms follow the minister in and stand side by side, each with his best man behind him. Cindy's groom stands nearer the aisle.

Cindy and Steve ascend the steps and take their place at the left side of the altar; Linda and Mike go to the right. The brides' father stands behind or below Cindy, and the man who escorted Linda goes to his seat in the first or second pew.

The service is read to both couples, but those parts that require responses are read twice. Cindy and Steve answer first. Their father gives both daughters away, Cindy first, Linda second. Then he takes his place with his wife in the first pew.

At the end of the ceremony, Cindy and Steve leave first. Linda and Mike follow them. The maids of honor follow, walking with the two best men. The bridesmaids and ushers pair off, the older couple's attendants going first.

Seating the Parents

When two sisters share a double-wedding ceremony, the only problem is in seating both grooms' parents. They must either agree to share the first pew on the right or they must draw lots for it.

In the event that the brides are not sisters, their two mothers should share the first pew, the older woman being given the seat nearer the aisle. Both fathers join them there, and the husband of the mother farther from the aisle must slip by the other in order to sit next to his own wife.

Reception for a Double Wedding

The sisters' mother—and their father, if he wishes—stands first in the receiving line. Next to them stand Cindy's mother-in-law and then Cindy and Steve, in whichever order puts her on his right. Mike's mother stands next, with Linda and Mike beside her. Cindy's maid of honor and then Linda's maid of honor join the line, but since there are already so many in it, the bridesmaids do not. For the same reason, it is just as well if the grooms' fathers wander about and chat with their friends. If the brides are not sisters, two separate receiving lines are formed.

When each couple has many attendants, it is better that they have separate bridal tables, close to or facing each other. If the parties are small, they may sit together at one long table. One couple would sit at either end, or in the center of each long side. Their own maids of honor and best men would be seated on their right and left, and the other attendants would alternate—either on the same long side as their own couple or at the same end where their couple is seated.

Each couple has its own cake. They cut the cakes one after the other so that each may watch the other's ceremony.

The three sets of parents sit together at the parents' table, if possible. The brides' mother must discuss with the grooms' families which close relatives should be invited to join them. If four sets of parents are involved, it is more comfortable to have two separate tables.

If matchboxes or napkins are monogrammed, both sets of initials or names are included.

Otherwise a double-wedding reception is identical to that of a single wedding.

Although invitations for a double wedding—when the brides are not sisters—are sent in the name of both brides' families (see page 89), announcements need not be. Each bride's mother may send the announcement of her own daughter's wedding, not mentioning the other at all.

The Working Couple's Wedding

If you and the groom are planning to go on working right up until the day of your wedding, and to return immediately after your honeymoon, you will necessarily have to cut down on the number of activities connected with it. You will also have to start your preparations earlier, since you will have only weekends and evenings to take care of them. Your mother may take on a number of chores for you, but it is not fair to burden her with all the decisions and all the labor. Instead, consider taking advantage of all the services available today. Bridal consultants in stores can save you hours of time by showing you bridal clothes by appointment. They can also help with the overall planning of the wedding. Other services that will help to take the load off your shoulders are the florist, the photographer, and, most of all, the caterer. To settle details with these people only takes a little time out of your day, and can be done at lunch hour or on a Saturday.

Even if you are having a large wedding, don't let too many attendants and friends plan parties. Try to restrict the festivities—luncheons, showers—to one a weekend or an occasional early after-work party.

If you work in a very small office, you may wish to invite all the staff, but in a large office you need invite only those who are really your friends. Your immediate superior should be invited, and his or her wife or husband is included. You may also invite close business associates of yours and the groom and their spouses, if you wish. If your wedding is very formal, each co-worker you invite should receive a separate invitation. Even for a less formal wedding, it is best to send separate invitations if you possibly can. But if your funds are strictly limited, or you are writing the invitations yourself, you can issue a blanket invitation. If you do this, address it to "The Staff" (or whatever is appropriate) and try to add an oral invitation to everyone.

This is also true when acknowledging a wedding gift sent by your co-workers together. You may send one thank-you note if you must, but add your personal spoken thanks as soon as you return to the office. Again, a personal note to each of the contributors is preferable.

Remember that both members of a couple are always included in an invitation. Therefore, if you post a single invitation for the staff, this means that all married ones may bring their husbands or wives if they wish to come, and this may make a larger group than you can cope with. Therefore think carefully, and if you are limited, invite only your one or two closest friends individually, in addition to your boss.

A Religious Service Following a Civil Ceremony

Frequently a couple who has been married by a justice of the peace wants to be married again in a church ceremony. This is a perfectly proper—in fact, a most desirable thing to do. However, the bride cannot make a pretense of its being her first wedding. She should not, for example, wear a veil, for that is the symbol of virginity. But if the religious ceremony takes place very shortly after the civil ceremony, she may have as many guests as she wishes, and there may be a reception complete with cake, music, and champagne.

In the event that considerable time has passed since the civil ceremony, the re-enactment of the marriage should be kept very simple. Relatives and close friends may attend, of course, but the ceremony, and the reception following—if there is one—should be intimate and dignified.

An alternative to an actual religious ceremony is the blessing of a civil marriage. There is such a service in *The Book of Common Worship.* It is similar to a marriage service, but the clergyman says, "Do you *acknowledge* this woman . . ." (rather than *take*) and makes other appropriate changes. No one gives the bride away, nor does she receive a ring for a second time. There are no attendants.

If the blessing follows soon after a civil ceremony, a reception may be held afterward, just as after any other wedding ceremony.

11

WHEN YOU'VE BEEN MARRIED BEFORE

Simplicity is the key for all second marriages. (Of course, this applies to third marriages also, or any marriage after the first one.) They may be as beautiful, as reverent, as meaningful as the first, but to be in the best of taste they should be dignified and simple. The fact that a groom has been married before, however, has no effect on the size or elegance of a bride's first wedding.

The First Wedding and Engagement Rings

Whether a woman continues to wear her wedding and engagement rings when her first marriage ends depends on many things. A widow almost always goes on wearing both until she decides to remarry. A divorcée usually removes both. If she has children, however, she may continue to wear her wedding ring to show her formerly married status. Some young widows and divorcées who wish to let it be known that they are not opposed to being married again transfer their rings to their right hands, which is perfectly acceptable. The one important rule is that the original engagement ring and the wedding ring (unless there are children involved) must be removed as soon as a woman decides to marry again.

The disposition of the old rings should be discussed with your prospective husband. If the engagement ring is valuable, it may be kept for a son to give to his future bride. If it contains five stones, those may be reset into a pin or clip for a daughter or, if your second husband has no objection, for yourself. It would seem a shame to put a beautiful piece of jewelry away and never use it unless it evokes painful memories or is a bone of contention in your new marriage.

Wedding rings are generally not very valuable. A widow may keep her first ring for sentimental reasons; a divorcée usually discards hers. If it is a diamond ring or one that has great value, the same treatment would be accorded it as described for the engagement ring.

The Second Wedding Ceremony

A widow's second marriage may take place in any of the places a first wedding takes place. A divorcée may be married in church if her faith permits it, or in her home or that of her parents or a friend, or she may simply be married in a civil ceremony by a judge or justice of the peace. In the last case, there need be no one present but the two necessary witnesses and possibly members of the immediate families.

In the past, brides being married for a second time never wore white. This has changed, and many second-time brides are wearing traditional, white wedding gowns. They still must not, however, wear a veil, unless demanded by religious custom; a gown with a train; or carry orange blossoms. For a very simple wedding, a short cocktail dress or suit in a pastel color is always in good taste. A young woman who is having a more elaborate wedding may wear a long dress in white, preferably with color in the trim and in her accessories, in off-white, or in a very pale color. The men may wear semiformal wedding attire or business suits.

A second-time bride usually does not have more than one or two attendants, and perhaps a small daughter serving as a flower girl. The maid of honor and bridesmaids' costumes should be in keeping with that of the bride. If enough guests are invited to the church to warrant it, the groom may have one or two ushers. She may have a processional and recessional, just as for a first wedding, or if the ceremony is more simple and guests fewer, the procession can be eliminated, with the bride, groom, maid of honor and best man merely coming in from a side room and standing in front of the minister when the ceremony is to begin.

The ceremony itself is exactly the same as that of a first wedding, whether held in a place of worship or at home, or another location. Some faiths do not permit a second marriage to take place in the church or temple if either party has been divorced, or for other reasons. These weddings, then, generally take place at home with an officiating minister, a justice of the peace, or, at times, a minister of a different faith. These are matters that must be discussed with your minister well in advance.

The Reception

The party is exactly like any other wedding reception. The bride, the groom, their parents, and the maid of honor form a receiving line if the party is large, just as for a first wedding. The location of the reception is determined, just as it is for a first wedding, by the formality of the occasion, the number of guests, the wishes of the bride and the groom, and their budget.

Invitations and Announcements

When the guest list for a second marriage is restricted to family members and close friends, it is not difficult to issue invitations by personal notes or even by telephone. When the guest list is large, invitation choices are the same as for a first wedding. The wording follows:

Mr. and Mrs. David Hillman
request the honour of your presence
at the marriage of their daughter
Amanda Hillman Peyton
to
(etc.)

An older widow, or a bride and groom who are giving their wedding themselves, may send out invitations in this form:

The honour of your presence
is requested
at the marriage of
Mrs. John Franklin Cavenaugh
to
(etc.)

[or]

Mrs. John Franklin Cavenaugh
and
Mr. Stewart Bellows Ronk
request the honour of your presence
at their marriage
(etc.)

A divorcée would use the same form except she would use her own first name and maiden name with her ex-husband's last name: "Mrs. Alexandra Hunt Osborn." If she had reverted to her maiden name after her divorce, she would naturally use her own first, middle and last names: "Alexandra Jane Hunt."

Whether engraved invitations are sent or not, it is correct for the bride or her parents to send as many engraved announcements of the marriage as they wish. When they are sent by the bride's parents, the form is exactly like that of a first wedding announcement, except that the bride's full name is used, as it was on the invitation.

A divorcée or a widow and her new husband may announce their marriage in this way:

> *Mrs. Alexandra Hunt Osborn* (divorcée)
> [or]
> *Mrs. Steven Phillip Osborn* (widow)
> *and*
> *Mr. Scott Francis Aabel*
> *announce their marriage*
> *on Saturday, the tenth of May*
> *(etc.)*

See Chapter 5 for additional examples of invitations and announcements.

The Role of Children by a First Marriage

Until a decade or so ago, it was considered to be in very poor taste to have children of a first marriage at the second. Fortunately this is no longer true; we realize that children will adjust to a new family far more quickly if they feel they are a part of the formation of that family. Therefore, unless it is their own wish not to attend, they should always be included. Depending on how comfortable they are with their mother's or father's upcoming marriage, they may be members of the wedding party or, if they are reluctant, they may attend with a favorite aunt or uncle, as guests.

An older bride may have her grown daughter as her attendant—an older male groom may have his son. When a divorce has occurred, however, children of the previous marriage should *never* be asked to serve as attendants without the first spouse's knowledge, especially if the children live with the first spouse. Not to discuss this first with the former spouse puts the children in a position of disloyalty to their other parent and may cause hurt for everyone. If many years have passed since the divorce took place and no contact has been maintained with the other parent, that is another matter. But if the children have remained close to both parents, the parents must communicate before the children are involved.

The Parents of a First Husband or Wife

Many people remain very close to the family of their first spouse. This is especially true if there are children from that marriage. The question of whether these parents-in-law, or former sisters- or brothers-in-law, should be invited to the second wedding of the man or woman who was previously part of their family by marriage, is one that must be settled according to the circumstances and the feelings of the people involved. The bride and the groom must discuss this first, and then, if neither has a problem with former in-laws being invited, the situation should be discussed with these former family members. They may be devoted to the bride or the groom, and thrilled at the prospect of his or her remarriage and the prospect of a new mother or father for their grandchildren. Or they may be filled with dismay at the thought of someone's replacing their son or daughter.

In either case, the bride and groom must consider whether it would create an embarrassing situation with the new family if the first in-laws attend. All I can say is that either solution is correct. You must simply do what seems best and will make everyone happiest in your own case.

12

GIFTS

In general, everyone who receives an invitation to a wedding reception or to a small wedding in a club, hotel, or at home sends a gift. An invitation to a church ceremony alone carries no such obligation. Neither does a wedding announcement.

Occasionally a bride's family will send invitations to both wedding and reception to everyone with whom they have the slightest acquaintance, even though they know some will not be able to or wish to come. This is in poor taste, since it seems an obvious bid for more gifts. Instead, the considerate bride sends announcements to those acquaintances so that they will feel no obligation. People receiving an invitation who barely know the bride, or perhaps have not seen her in years, should feel no compunction in refusing it, nor need they send a present.

An older bride, or one being married for the second time, often has all the furnishings she can use, and she and her groom really do not want any gifts. She does, however, expect gifts from her family and her closest friends, as well as from the groom's closest friends. If the groom has not been married before, his friends and relatives will undoubtedly send gifts.

It is not in good taste to write "No gifts please" on wedding invitations, but the bride may ask family and close friends to help her spread the word. If she and her future husband are deeply interested in a cause or a charity, she could write on the invitations, "In lieu of gifts, we would greatly appreciate a contribution to the Leukemia Society."

Gifts from Family and Friends

All close members of your family and your groom's family will naturally want to send gifts, whether they attend the wedding or not. The bride's parents often start her flat-silver service with as many place settings as they can afford. Your fiancé's mother and father may give you china or crystal or furnishings for your home—your beds or your living-room furniture, for example. One family or the other may give you a check to help with a new home or the honeymoon expenses, but for sentimental reasons a gift that will forever be in evidence, and enjoyed, has more value.

Bridal Registries

One of the things you should be sure to do before you send out your invitations is to go to the bridal registries of your local gift and department stores to select and list with them your choices of china, silver, and crystal patterns and indicate which pieces you would like to have. You may also make selections from any of the other articles they have in stock. You should pick out individual items in as wide a range of prices as you possibly can. Then, when someone asks you what you would like as a present, you need only say, "I have listed a number of choices at the X and Y stores. If you'll stop by, they will be glad to show you the things I've chosen." If your friend cannot get to those stores, try to help by suggesting the *type* of gift you would like rather than a specific article. For example, you can say, "I really prefer pewter to silver," or "We're furnishing our living room in Early American," or "We love gardening, so anything for our yard (or terrace) would be great."

For information about monogramming, see chapter 2.

The Gift List

Several weeks before the wedding, you should either make or buy a book in which to keep a record of your wedding gifts. Should a member of your family ask what you would like for a present, one of these specially designed books is an ideal answer. They are usually set up in this way:

No.	Present Received	Article	Sent by	Sender's Address	Where Bought	Thanks Written
11.	6/20	Silver Platter	Mr. and Mrs. White	Glenwood Road Peekskill, N.Y. 10969	Tiffany	6/21
12.	6/21	8 cresent salad plates	Aunt Helen	12 Loew Street Albany, N.Y. 12159	Gamble's Gift Shop	6/21

The books often come with sheets of numbered stickers. As soon as each gift is opened a number is pasted to the bottom and the item is entered beside the corresponding number in the book. A sticker goes on only one item of each design—one of a dozen plates, for example.

Thank-You Notes

For every present received, whether the bride has thanked the donor in person or not, she must write a thank-you note, except to her immediate family and her very closest friends.

The wise bride writes her notes on the day the presents arrive for as long as she can keep up. Since the majority of gifts will arrive in the last few days before the wedding, she will undoubtedly fall behind then, but the more that have been answered, the less she will have to do after the honeymoon. In ordinary circumstances, all thank-you notes should be sent within three months of the date of the wedding.

In the unusual event that a bride or groom is so prominent that the couple receives a staggering number of gifts, a printed or engraved card may be sent out, to be followed as soon as possible by the bride's personal note. This also can be done by the bride's mother when the couple goes away for an extended time, so that the friends who sent the gifts know that they were received. Cards sent before the wedding must bear the bride's maiden name. In the second case, they would undoubtedly be sent after the marriage, so they should bear her married name.

> *Mrs. John Hancock*
> *acknowledges with thanks*
> *the receipt of your wedding gift*
> *and will write you a personal note*
> *as soon as possible*

Thank-you notes should be written on notepaper. It may be plain or bordered paper, in a conservative color, or it may be monogrammed. A foresighted bride orders her paper some weeks before the wedding, some with her maiden initials for thank-you notes sent before the ceremony, and the rest with her married initials for notes sent after the wedding and for future use.

Thank-you notes are signed by the bride because presents are usually sent to her, but a reference in the text to her husband makes the note more friendly. When a gift arrives from a relative or friend of the groom, addressed to him and his bride, he may write the note if he wishes. However, in most cases, this duty

Sample Bridal/Gift Registry Card

Name Here

BRIDAL REGISTRY AND GIFT RECORD

Bride _____ Wedding Date _____

Bride's Address _____ Send gifts to (address) _____

Bride's Phone: Res. _____ Bus. _____ Groom's Phone _____ Other _____

Date Registered _____ Registered Elsewhere (if yes, indicate where) _____

Overall Color Preference: _____ Kitchen Color _____ Bath Color _____

GIFT REGISTRY

Name _____ Phone _____

Birthdays: Wife _____ Anniversary _____

Overall Color Preference: _____ Kitchen Color _____ Bath Color _____

Style Preference of Rooms _____

FORMAL PATTERNS

CHINA Pattern	Mfr.	Dept.	Class Bride Wants	Date Rec'd
DINNER PLATE				
SALAD				
BREAD & BUTTER				
CUP & SAUCER				
SOUP				
PLATTERS				
GRAVY BOAT				
VEGETABLE DISH				
OTHER:				

CRYSTAL Pattern	Mfr.	Dept.	Class Bride Wants	Date Rec'd
GOBLET				
CHAMPAGNE (flute or saucer)				
RED WINE				
WHITE WINE				
ICED BEVERAGE				
BRANDY				
SHERRY				
CORDIAL				
PITCHER				
OTHER:				

FLATWARE—silver or silverplate Pattern	Mfr.	Dept.	Class Bride Wants	Date Rec'd
TEASPOON				
KNIFE				
FORK				
SALAD FORK				
PLACE SPOON				
BUTTER SPREADER				
TABLESPOON				
SUGAR SPOON				
COLD MEAT FORK				
OTHER:				

INFORMAL PATTERNS

CASUAL DINNERWARE Pattern	Mfr.	Dept.	Class Bride Wants	Date Rec'd
DINNER PLATE				
SALAD				
BREAD & BUTTER				
CUP & SAUCER				
SOUP				
PLATTERS				
GRAVY BOAT				
VEGETABLE DISH				
OTHER:				

INFORMAL GLASSWARE/BARWARE Pattern	Mfr.	Dept.	Class Bride Wants	Date Rec'd
GOBLET				
CHAMPAGNE (flute or saucer)				
RED WINE				
WHITE WINE				
ICED BEVERAGE				
HIGHBALL				
OLD-FASHIONED				
DOUBLE OLD-FASHIONED				
MARTINI				
OTHER:				

FLATWARE—stainless Pattern	Mfr.	Dept.	Class Bride Wants	Date Rec'd
TEASPOON				
KNIFE				
FORK				
SALAD FORK				
PLACE SPOON				
BUTTER SPREADER				
TABLESPOON				
SUGAR SPOON				
COLD MEAT FORK				
OTHER:				

Name Here

KITCHEN EQUIPMENT

Pattern/Color	Mfr.	Dept.	Class Bride Wants	Date Rec'd
BAKING DISH				
CANISTER SET				
CUTLERY SET				
CUTTING BOARD				
COVERED CASSEROLE _____ QT.				
COVERED CASSEROLE _____ QT.				
DOUBLE BOILER				
FOOD PROCESSOR				
GADGETS				
KITCHEN TOOL SET				
SAUCEPAN _____ QT.				
SAUCEPAN _____ QT.				
SAUCEPAN _____ QT.				
SKILLET _____ IN.				
SKILLET _____ IN.				
SKILLET _____ IN.				
TEA KETTLE				
WOK				
OTHER:				

TABLE & KITCHEN LINENS

Pattern/Color	Mfr. (size)	Dept.	Class Bride Wants	Date Rec'd
TABLE				
CLOTHS				
NAPKINS				
PLACEMATS				
KITCHEN LINENS				
APPLIANCE COVERS				
APRONS				
HOT PADS				
MITTS				
POTHOLDERS				
TOWELS				
OTHER:				

MISCELLANEOUS

Pattern/Color	Mfr.	Dept.	Class Bride Wants	Date Rec'd
DECORATIVE ACCESSORIES				
BASKETS				
BOWLS				
CANDLESTICKS				
CLOCKS				
FIGURINES				
MIRRORS				
PILLOWS				
WALL DECOR				
OTHER:				
FASHION LUGGAGE				
CARRY-ONS				
DUFFLES				
GARMENT BAGS				
TOTE				
PERSONAL LEATHER GOODS (wallets, passport cases, etc.)				

PAPER GOODS/STATIONERY CHOICES

DESCRIPTION/MFR.	NO.	PRICE	ITEM/DESCRIPTION	DATE PURCH.
ANNOUNCEMENTS				
INVITATIONS				
RECEPTION CARDS				
RESPONSE CARDS				
ADDRESS BOOK				
BRIDE'S FILE				
COCKTAIL NAPKINS				
DINNER NAPKINS				
GUEST BOOK				
GUEST TOWELS				
INFORMALS				
PERSONALIZED MATCHES				
PERSONAL STATIONERY				
PHOTO ALBUM				
THANK-YOU NOTES				
WEDDING BOOK				
WEDDING PROGRAM				
OTHER:				

GIFT REGISTRY CHOICES

ITEM/DESCRIPTION	PRICE	DATE PURCH.

falls to the bride. When a gift comes from a couple, the note can be addressed to the wife, but again a reference to the husband is friendly—"We want to thank you and Mr. Hennessy so much. . . ." Or, if you prefer, you may address your letter to "Mr. and Mrs. Hennessy" and use that salutation.

Your note should include a reference to the present itself, not just a general thanks. It need not be long, but a special word or two about the gift shows your appreciation. Above all, your sincerity must come through. The following examples may give you some ideas.

TO A CLOSE FAMILY FRIEND

Dear Mrs. French,

It was just great of you to send us all those beautiful wineglasses! Brian and I both thank you a thousand times, and hope you will have dinner with us soon to join us in christening them.

Our presents will be on display during the week before the wedding, so please stop by for a cup of coffee and an early "viewing."

Affectionately,
Kate

MORE FORMALLY

Dear Mr. and Mrs. Knight,

The clock you sent us is such a thoughtful gift. We look forward to seeing you both on the 27th, and in the meantime, thank you so much.

Very sincerely,
Elizabeth Newberry

FOR A PRESENT RECEIVED AFTER THE WEDDING

Dear Aunt Blanche,

The mirror you sent us just fits the space over the mantel, and we needed it desperately. It goes beautifully with our decorating scheme.

Please stop by soon and see how lovely it looks—we would like to thank you in person.

Affectionately,
Susan

Dear Uncle Jerry,

Your check came as a welcome surprise. Kate and I have put it into the fund for our living-room sofa, and we will think of you often when it finally arrives.

We were so sorry you could not make the wedding, but hope to see you soon.

With love from us both,
Brian

Thank-You Notes with Pictures

I would like to include a word here about the custom of sending a thank-you card that has a picture of the bride and groom on it. It makes a most attractive memento of the wedding and is especially nice for friends who could not attend. However, there are two serious drawbacks. First, since the pictures cannot be taken until the wedding day, and days—even weeks—may elapse before they are printed, it may be some time before the cards can be sent. Friends who rightfully feel that promptness is important in acknowledging wedding presents may get quite upset at the delay. Second, some brides feel that because the card carries a printed thank-you message, they need not add to it. This is inexcusable. The bride *must* add her personal message, including a reference to the specific gift and an indication of her sincere gratitude.

These cards are sold by your photographer and ordered at the time you arrange for these services. If you request the type of slotted card into which pictures can be easily inserted, you can have the cards at once, so that you may write your notes as the gifts arrive. Insist on receiving the prints for the cards as fast as possible—before the portraits or candid shots. Since you will be away on your honeymoon when proofs are ready, ask your mother or your maid of honor to select the best one at once. Then, as soon as the finished pictures arrive, they may be inserted and the cards mailed immediately, resulting in the least possible delay.

Displaying Wedding Presents

If you have the space—and the inclination—nothing could be nicer than to display your gifts. Your friends will enjoy seeing them, and you and your groom will have fun planning their use, comparing, discussing, and so on.

Gifts should be displayed at home only—never in a hotel or club. Any room of your house will do—a guest bedroom, a den, the dining room, or any space that can be spared in the days before the wedding. If the reception is not to be held at home, so that the guests will not see the presents on your wedding day, it is thoughtful to invite relatives and good friends to a cocktail or tea party a few days before the ceremony in order to show them your gifts.

The table or tables are covered with a white cloth. It may be damask or linen, or it may be a plain white sheet which may be decorated with artificial flowers or loops or bows of ribbon. If the sheet or tablecloth is allowed to hang to the floor, empty cartons, and the boxes containing those parts of sets which are not on display, may be stored underneath.

Although many people like to display all the silver on one table, all the china on another, and so on, I think presents look better when tastefully mixed. By doing so you can disguise the fact that you received eight silver candlesticks or three cake servers. Also, it avoids the possibility of inviting comparisons between an expensive solid silver pitcher and one of inferior quality. Try to group colors and materials carefully so that they will not clash but will complement each other.

Only one article of a set is displayed. If you receive eight glass dessert plates, only one is put out on the table. One complete place setting correctly displays your silver service. The same is true of your china. When the gift consists of a pair of candlesticks, however, both are shown.

If you expect to receive a large number of valuable gifts, it is a good idea to hire a private detective or an off-duty policeman to watch your house when everyone has left for the church. The empty house, with tables of silverware and valuable appliances in clear view, is an open invitation to thieves.

Cards Displayed with Presents

There is no definite rule about displaying cards. Some people like to do so, to relieve members of the family of having to answer innumerable questions of "Who gave this?" or "What did Aunt Katie send?" On the other hand, some families feel that leaving the cards displayed leads to odious comparisons. They also feel that it is a private matter between the bride and her friends. So it is up to you.

Checks as Wedding Gifts

Checks given as wedding presents may be displayed with the other gifts; they definitely should be if you have decided to display cards. They should be laid on the table, overlapping so that the name at the bottom shows but the amount does not. The amount written on the top check is covered. A piece of clear glass should be laid over them to keep them from blowing away, or to prevent curious guests from taking a peek.

When checks are sent as gifts before the wedding takes place, they are generally made out to both bride and groom—Katherine Adams and Brian Jamison. If, however, a grandparent or relative prefers, the check may be made out to either member of the couple. Checks made out to both may be deposited in a joint account, or, if signed by both, may be deposited in either the bride's or the groom's own account.

Checks delivered at the reception, or sent to the couple after the ceremony, are made out to both—Katherine and Brian Jamison—when the bride changes her name. If she does not the check is made out as it would be before the wedding—Katherine Adams and Brian Jamison.

Delivery of Gifts

Gifts are usually sent to the bride's house before the day of the wedding, addressed to her maiden name. When they are sent after the wedding takes place, they go to Mr. and Mrs. Jamison at their new address, or in care of the bride's family.

In some localities and among certain ethnic groups it is customary to take checks or gifts to the wedding reception. When this is done, they are usually given to the bride as the guest goes through the receiving line or, with some ethnic groups, during a farewell to the bride and groom. Checks are put into a bag or receptacle held by the bride, and gifts are piled on a table nearby. The bride and groom open them at a later date, so that they can enjoy their dining and dancing at the reception as well as the company of their guests.

Exchanging Presents

It is perfectly permissible to exchange a duplicate present for something else. Whether or not you inform the donor of your action is entirely up to you. If you know her very well, you will probably wish to tell her; if she is merely an acquaintance, you may simply write and thank her for her original gift. Friends should never feel hurt when a bride chooses to make an exchange—no sensible person would expect her to keep twenty salts and peppers or seven mirrors.

Gifts are *never* returned to the donor unless the wedding is actually canceled. If it is merely postponed, the gifts are kept for the future marriage.

When the Wedding Plans Change

When a wedding is called off at the last moment the gifts must be returned as soon as possible. If it is merely delayed, perhaps owing to illness or a death in the family, they need not be returned, even though some time elapses before the ceremony takes place.

Broken Gifts

When a gift arrives broken or damaged, the bride should, if possible, take or send it back to the store from which it came. All reputable stores will gladly replace merchandise broken in delivery. If the gift does not come directly from a store, the bride should look on the wrapping to see if it is insured. If so, she should notify the sender at once, so that he or she can collect the insurance money and replace it. If it is not insured, the bride must decide whether or not she should mention the situation to the donor. Since the latter would surely feel obligated to replace the broken article, in most instances it is better that the bride merely send her thanks and say nothing. Only when the person sending the gift is a close friend who would soon notice that it is not in evidence should the matter be brought up.

Gifts for Attendants

The groom gives his best man and each usher a gift, and the bride does the same for her attendants. The bride's gifts are usually presented at the bridesmaids' luncheon, if there is one. If not, they may be given at any time she sees them, or at the rehearsal dinner. The groom delivers his gifts at the bachelor dinner or the rehearsal dinner.

The most suitable gifts are items of jewelry which can be marked with the date and the initials of the bride and groom. They may also be such things as wallets or leather belts for the ushers, or picture frames, or a memento such as a charm for the bridesmaids.

13

FLOWERS, DECORATIONS, AND MUSIC

The flowers for a wedding may be as simple as a single rose carried by the bride or as elaborate as bouquets for the bride and each of her attendants. Regardless, the flowers should be in keeping with the character and formality of the wedding.

Bridal Party Flowers

The bride should wait until she has selected her wedding gown and those of her attendants before placing the precise order for their bouquets, and should, if possible, have a picture of the gowns and fabric swatches to enable the florist to make the most appropriate recommendations. Flowers carried by the bride and her attendants are an accessory which must complement the gowns and contribute to the overall look of the wedding. A cascading bouquet, for example, looks best with a long gown. It appears out of proportion with a shorter dress. A small nosegay, on the other hand, is too small against a long gown with a train, but looks well with a short dress or a simple suit. You should have the mood you want to convey in mind as well, whether Victorian, exotic, sophisticated or traditional. You must decide if you want a colorful bouquet or one entirely in white. Either is lovely, but both should include a combination of flowers in a variety of sizes to give balance.

The texture of your and your bridesmaids' gowns is important, too. Camellias and gardenias with their shiny dark leaves are beautiful against a satin or brocade dress. Eyelet and cotton are better complemented by daisies or sweet peas. Chrysanthemums, stock, or carnations carry out the fluffier look of tulle or organza. Calla lilies, large orchids, and gladioli are good choices for a tall bride; tinier blossoms—lilies of the valley, violets, sweetheart roses—arranged in a smaller bouquet or cascade are better for the petite bride.

White orchids are generally arranged with other flowers. Orchids are a "formal" flower and therefore look best with a formal wedding gown. An arrangement or orchids is appropriate for decorating a prayer book or a satin purse. Calla lilies are possibly the most formal of all bridal flowers. They are stunning when carried by a bride wearing a satin or velvet gown with simple lines. They are often arranged against a background of dark, shiny leaves to provide contrast.

A bouquet may be made up so that the center flowers may be removed and worn by the bride as a corsage when she leaves for her honeymoon. The remainder of the bouquet is thrown to the bridesmaids, as described in Chapter 10. Sometimes a bride who wants to keep and preserve her own bouquet will order another, "tossing" bouquet for this tradition.

Formal Bouquets

If the style of your wedding is formal with long gowns for you and your attendants, you might choose either a cascade or a crescent styling with a draped effect. Orchids, roses, gardenias, camellias, stephanotis, lilies of the valley, and

other lilies are lovely choices for more formal bouquets, complemented by seasonal flowers. A large nosegay or a free form bouquet of formal flowers can also be a lovely choice.

If your gown has waistline detailing, a crescent bouquet or an over-arm bouquet that won't cover waistline beading or appliqué would be a good choice.

A shiny satin or brocade gown is well-complemented by flowers with shiny, dark green leaves such as camellias and gardenias.

Informal Bouquets

If your wedding is less formal, a loose garden bouquet is appropriate. Garden flower bouquets could include tulips, freesia, irises, astors, small daisies and roses, or a selection of seasonal fall blossoms for an autumn wedding. Other choices would include a nosegay or oval-shaped arrangement, or one or a few seasonal flowers wrapped with a ribbon. Daisies, violets, roses, and other smaller flowers can make a beautiful bouquet.

Attendants' Bouquets

Usually the maid of honor carries the same bouquet as the bridesmaids, although her special role may be highlighted by using different, complementary colors of the same flowers or a different style. Attendants' flowers should be of a similar style and mood to those of the bride.

Floral Headpieces

Flowers worn in the hair of the bride's attendants should be ordered with the bouquets so that they are well-coordinated. Be sure to choose long lasting flowers that will not wilt during the ceremony and reception. They may wear a wreath of flowers, or just a few flowers attached to a comb to be worn at the back or side of the head. The bride may also wear flowers in her hair in lieu of a hat or a veil, or they may be attached to the veil. If this is the case, the veiling should be given to the florist. You might consider using silk flowers for headpieces, identical or complementary to the real flowers used in the bouquets. Most florists carry silk flowers and are able to create headpieces for you.

Flowers for the Flower Girl

A child attendant should carry a delicate bouquet—either a miniature version of those of the bridesmaids or one more suited to her size in complementary flowers. Often flower girls carry a small basket of flowers instead of a bouquet.

Corsages

Once the color and style of the bride's and groom's mothers, and stepmothers, has been determined, coordinating corsages should be ordered for them. It is thoughtful to ask them if they have a favorite flower and if they prefer a corsage to be pinned at the shoulder, waist, or handbag, or to be worn on the wrist. Flowers for grandmothers should be something rather neutral, such as clusters of tiny white orchids or a single gardenia—something in a creamy color that will be complementary to any dress. In addition, a small floral accessory, such as a corsage or a flower for the wrist, may be given to a friend who attends the guest book and to a friend who serves as a soloist during the ceremony.

The Groom's Boutonniere

Select one flower from your bouquet for your groom's boutonniere. Often this is stephanotis, lily of the valley or another smaller flower. This tradition comes from a romantic custom of yesteryear when the bride would remove one blossom from her bouquet and pin it on her groom as a symbol of her love.

Other Boutonnieres

Ushers, other groomsmen, fathers and often grandfathers all wear boutonnieres. Brothers of the bride or groom who are not in the wedding may wear a boutonniere, as well, which is a very nice way to show them that they are important to you. These boutonnieres should be different than that of the groom's, and may be a single carnation or another flower selected from the bridesmaids' bouquets.

Ceremony Decorations

Flowers for the ceremony are as elaborate or as simple as you choose. Your minister's or rabbi's advice can be most helpful in choosing those for the altar and chancel, or for the chuppah, pulpit and candelabra. Whether or not you have flowers on the ends of the pews depends on the size and formality of the wedding. If your florist is not familiar with the site of the wedding, it would be helpful if he or she visited the site before your consultation to know which size and style of floral arrangements best suit the location.

These flowers may be all white with greens, or they may be bright or pastel colors. Either is appropriate, as long as they complement the colors of the site and of the clothing worn by the bridal party.

If your guest list is small but your church or synagogue is large and no chapel is available, you can counteract the feeling of emptiness by placing a hedge of potted plants or a row of greens along the back of the last pew to be used, forming a border. The part within the boundary is brilliantly lighted—the rest of the church or synagogue relatively dark. The bridal party, rather than walking down a long, dimly lit aisle, would enter from a side door. Another alternative, even simpler, is to use chancel choir stalls for guests, lighting only that section of the church.

A candlelight ceremony in the evening or very late afternoon can be very beautiful with ivy twined around the candelabra and white satin bows decorating the ends of the pews. If you prefer, flowers, greens and candles may be used together, but do not overdo the flowers, or the result will be confused and give the appearance of a hodgepodge of elements.

You should discuss with your minister or rabbi what you would like done with ceremony flowers after the service. They may be left behind if there is to be a service the next day, or they may be delivered to special friends or relatives who are infirm and unable to attend your wedding. They may also be delivered to a hospital or nursing home so they can be enjoyed. Often your florist, for an additional fee, will take care of this for you, or a church or synagogue member will make these deliveries, at the request of the minister, priest, or rabbi.

Decorations for a Home Wedding

There are so many variables in weddings at home that it is almost impossible to describe the decorations. In general, they consist of a screen or backdrop of greens or a dark drapery behind the improvised altar, and vases of flowers in the windows, on newel posts, and on occasional tables. If the room has a fireplace, this makes an ideal setting for the ceremony. The fireplace may be filled with greens, and the mantel decorated with green roping or an arrangement of greens or flowers.

An altar may easily be made up by covering an ordinary table with a white silk, lace, or damask cloth, or by an altar cloth borrowed from your church. Whether or not there is a cross or other religious objects on the altar depends on the service, on your faith, and on the officiating clergyman. More commonly there is simply a kneeling bench for the couple, possibly with an altar rail behind it, covered with greens or a drapery. A tall stand containing a flower arrangement at each end of the rail makes a lovely frame for the ceremony.

If the house is large enough to permit it, stanchions decorated with flowers may be used to support the ribbon marking an aisle to the altar. This is not necessary, but it adds to the beauty and elegance of a home ceremony.

Flowers for the home wedding, then, are used in whatever profusion and whatever manner the bride will enjoy—and her pocketbook will permit.

Decorations and Frills for Receptions

Decorations for receptions invariably consist of flowers and greens, generally white but often white mixed with colors, or pastel shades chosen to blend with the colors of the bridal party.

A buffet table may have a bowl of flowers as its centerpiece, or, if space is limited, the center of the table may be used for the wedding cake. Often, when there is a seated-bridal-party table, the cake is placed in front of the bride and groom. If the cake is tall, however, it is better to put a low flower arrangement there, so that the bridal couple is not hidden from the guests. Depending on the length and shape of the table, there may be one or two more arrangements at each side. Candles or candelabra may be used at an evening or after-dusk reception but should not be on the tables for a morning or early-afternoon reception.

When the guests are served a sit-down dinner, there are generally small flower arrangements on each table. At less formal receptions, even though there may be tables where the guests form their own groups to rest or enjoy the buffet, there need not be centerpieces. However, if the cost is not too great, flowers on every table add greatly to the beauty of the scene.

Other than the flowers on the tables, the only decoration is a bank of greens against which the receiving line is formed. Or the bridal party may stand in front of a fireplace, decorated with nothing more than a bowl of flowers at each end. When there is no focal point in a room, the line may be formed against the longest unbroken wall space, and a tall stanchion topped with a vase of flowers may be placed at either end.

At many large weddings there are mementos for the guests. White match-boxes with the bride and groom's names printed on them in gold or silver, or cocktail napkins marked in the same way, are most frequently seen. Years ago, favors were baked into the wedding cake, and some lucky guests went home with tiny charms—a thimble, a ring, or a wedding bell, perhaps—as a reminder of the occasion. This practice has become too expensive in recent years and is rarely seen today.

Music for the Religious Ceremony

To me, a wedding is not a wedding unless the procession enters the church to the strains of Wagner's "Wedding March" ("Here Comes the Bride") and leaves the church to the stirring tune of Mendelssohn's "Wedding March" from his *Midsummer Night's Dream.* However, some churches consider that this music is too secular, and some brides have their own special favorites that they wish to have played instead. There are many triumphal hymns or marches of a more religious nature that may be substituted for the traditional processional and recessional. Your organist will help you choose selections for a church ceremony. If you are being married at home, and plan to use records or tapes for music, ask your organist or choirmaster for suggestions and then listen to the pieces in your local music store before making your choice.

At a church ceremony, organ music is almost always played while the guests assemble. The selections should be joyous, but they may not be "popular" music. In most churches, such traditional love songs as "I Love You Truly" or "Oh, Promise Me" are acceptable as background music, but in others they are not considered suitable. They have also become trite from overuse, and there are many other more original and more religious choices. A selected list might include:

"Jesu, Joy of Man's Desiring" by Bach
"Ave Maria" by Schubert
Chorale Prelude, "In Thee Is Joy" by Bach
"The Lord's Prayer" by Malotte
"Liebestraum" by Liszt
"Biblical Songs" by Dvořák
"Joyful, Joyful, We Adore Thee" by Beethoven
"The King of Love My Shepherd Is" by Hinsworth

Most of these are also excellent choices for a soloist. If you are having a choir sing at your wedding, choose the music with the help of the choir master.

Music at the Reception

Music at the reception may be provided by anything from a ten-piece band to a record or tape player. At some very formal weddings there are two orchestras, one playing rock or country music for the young people and the other playing more conventional music for the older guests. At other receptions, a strolling accordionist or guitarist provides the background music. The choice is yours, but no matter how small and simple the party, music in some form adds greatly to the festivity. The selections are up to you and your groom. A steady diet of loud modern music is not appropriate, as it is distasteful to many of the older guests, but if you have a dance orchestra, the softer, slower tunes should be interspersed with current favorites. The bride and groom usually dance their first dance to a traditional tune, even though they may enjoy more modern numbers later. The popularity of any piece of music changes so fast that it would be impossible to recommend specific songs. Make your own choice, but give due consideration to the preferences of your guests as well as to your own favorites.

14

MENU SUGGESTIONS

The following menus may be used in any combination that appeals to you. You may, of course, add your own favorite dishes or omit any items you do not like. But by combining several of these suggestions and adding your own flair, you will come up with some interesting and exciting meals.

While I have suggested serving champagne with most of the menus, it is entirely up to you whether you wish to do so or not. Many people serve no alcoholic beverages at all, and there are dozens of recipes for fruit punch, which makes a delicious substitute. Other people simply do not like champagne and prefer to serve cocktails or whiskey in long drinks instead. If you do serve liquor, it is essential that you also serve a fruit punch or soft drinks for those who do not drink alcohol.

If you feel that you would like to have other drinks as well as champagne available, it is perfectly correct to have a bar arranged with as many varieties of liquor as you care to offer. However, this can become very expensive and is not necessary. Champagne is the traditional wedding drink, and your guests will probably enjoy it more if there is no other choice.

Wedding Receptions

The Small Wedding Reception at Home

Frequently a wedding reception consists merely of a few friends or relatives invited to the bride's home after the ceremony. This is often true after a second marriage, or when the bride is older and has her own home. It is the simplest, least formal type of reception, but even so, the menu should be carefully planned and as beautifully prepared as possible.

[1]
Warm-Weather Menu

Cold curried pea soup
Open-face finger sandwiches
Tiny pastries filled with seafood
Thin cucumber slices between mayonnaise-coated rounds of very thin white bread
Bowls of assorted berries
Wedding cake
White wine   Punch, with or without liquor   Champagne
Coffee and tea

[2]
Cold-Weather Menu

Miniature Chinese-style chicken-wings with mustard and plum sauce
Sausage baked in a brioche
Broiled mushrooms with snail butter
Terrine of chicken liver
Fruit salad
Wedding cake
Champagne   Punch   Coffee and tea

[3]
Dips and Snacks

Taramasalata (Greek-style caviar dip) served with pita bread
Crudités (raw or lightly blanched vegetables) with an aïoli sauce (garlic or curry mayonnaise)
Platter of cheeses
Platter of cold meats
Breads
Wedding cake
Champagne   Coffee

The following menus are planned for a semiformal wedding reception at home or at a club, when the meal is served as a buffet. The three menus give you wide choice in both cost and elegance.

[1]

Individual picnic baskets for each guest, lined with
a checkered napkin and filled with food:

Cold chicken　　Cheese

Cherry tomatoes　　Fruit

Bread　　Small iced cakes

A bottle of wine

[2]

Lobster salad

Chicken in champagne sauce

Rice pilaf

Sautéed sugar-snap peas

Mixed green salad

Dinner rolls

Ice cream in a tulip-shaped cookie

Wedding cake

Champagne　　Tea　　Coffee

[3]

Cream of artichoke soup

Poached scallops in a cream sauce

Roast squab with a dried-fruit stuffing

Straw potatoes

Gratin of zucchini and tomatoes

Green salad

Rolls

Cassis sherbet

Wedding cake

Champagne　　Coffee　　Tea

The Seated Dinner

The seated wedding dinner is often very simple. The guests may be only the relatives and friends who attend the ceremony and return to the bride's home for a meal, or accompany the newlyweds to a restaurant. The first menu may be easily prepared at home; the others are somewhat more complicated and should be prepared by a caterer or in a restaurant or hotel. Naturally, the caterer or manager of the club or restaurant must be consulted well in advance. It is wise to follow their recommendations, as they will suggest the menus that they prepare best and which have proved to be most popular.

The first menu may be prepared by the bride or her family in advance, and the curry need only be heated for a few minutes when the party returns from the ceremony.

[1]

Melon with prosciutto

Curry of chicken

Rice

String beans amandine or buttered peas

Rolls

Grapefruit sherbet

Wedding cake

Champagne or white wine

Coffee and tea

[2]

Artichokes in a mustard vinaigrette sauce

Chicken chasseur

[*or*]

Boeuf bourguignon

Fresh noodles

Asparagus mimosa

French bread

Assorted berries with crême fraiche and caramel

Wedding cake

Red and white wines   Champagne   Coffee and tea

[3]

Consommé with sherry

Beef Wellington with a Périgord sauce

Braised endive

Purée of peas

Potatoes Anna

Green salad

Fruit compote with Kirschwasser or brandy

Wedding cake

Champagne   White and red wines

Tea   Coffee

While all wedding receptions held before evening used to be called "break-fasts," the custom seems to be going out of style. Now, when we hear the term, we generally think of a true breakfast held after a morning wedding. The bridal party almost invariably is seated, and often the guests are too, as the foods are not easy to eat buffet-style. The menus for an early wedding are simply those for an elaborate breakfast.

[1]
Broiled grapefruit halves
Canadian bacon with scrambled eggs
Brioche   Croissants   Cornbread
Wedding cake
Champagne   Coffee and tea

[2]
Cold peach soup
Eggs Benedict
Crêpes with choice of fillings: mushroom, apple, lingonberries
Croissants   Fruit muffins
Wedding cake
Champagne   Coffee and tea

[3]
Baked apples
Assortment of herrings in various sauces (curry, dill, wine)
Toast   Breads
Blueberry pancakes with blueberry sauce
Bacon   Fried ham
Wedding cake
Champagne   Coffee and Tea

A Morning Coffee or Brunch Shower

This section is for the bridesmaid who is planning to give a shower. Or you, the bride, may want to have some of your friends or your mother's friends in some morning to see your presents, and one of these menus will make their visit very special.

[1]

Wine cassis

Warm crabmeat dip

Fritto misto (batter-fried vegetables: onions, cauliflower, broccoli, eggplant,
tomatoes)

Scrambled eggs

Coffeecake   Toast   Rolls

Coffee and tea

[2]

A Mexican-style brunch

Bloody Marys

Sliced oranges with powdered sugar and cinnamon

Huevos rancheros (eggs with tortillas and hot tomato sauce)

Refried beans

Nachos

Mangoes and pineapple with dark rum and sugar

[3]

Dried fruit compote

Creamed finnan haddie

Broiled tomatoes

Steamed new potatoes

Biscuits   Popovers

Coffee and tea

[4]

White wine or champagne

Melon or strawberries

Grilled kippers

Corned beef hash with poached eggs

Sliced tomatoes

Toast   Scones   Muffins

Coffee and tea

Luncheons

The bride may give a luncheon for her bridesmaids, or they for her. Her
mother's friends or members of the bridal party often give her luncheon showers.

Any one of the following menus is appropriate, depending on the size and formality of the party. If cocktails are served, Bloody Marys, Daiquiris, and Dubonnet are popular. Iced tea and/or iced coffee should accompany warm-weather luncheons; hot coffee and tea should always be offered during or after luncheons in cool weather.

[1]

A Summer Luncheon

Cold cream of sorrel soup
Salade Niçoise (composed salad of lettuce, tomatoes, French potato salad, string beans, tuna fish, anchovies, hard-boiled eggs, black olives with a vinaigrette dressing)
French bread
Ice cream and cookies

[2]

Cold tomato and dill soup
Spinach quiche
Cold vegetables with herb mayonnaise
Peaches with raspberry sauce

[3]

Cold marinated mushrooms
Pâté in a crust
Potato salad
Mixed green salad
Chocolate brownies with vanilla ice cream

[4]

Cream of tomato soup
Poached eggs Florentine
Onion and orange salad
Bread and butter pudding

Afternoon Tea Showers

Tea menus basically consist of sandwiches, cookies, and cakes. You may let your imagination run wild in preparing unusual combinations, but remember sandwiches must be thin, the bread very fresh, and they should be tiny enough to be eaten in one or two bites. The two menus which follow are intended to suggest a range of ideas for summer and winter, but you will want to add your own variations and your own favorites.

[1]
A Summer Tea

Sliced turkey with cranberry/orange relish on small biscuits
Chicken salad (or shrimp salad) on finger rolls
Cold ratatouille in tart shells
Pâté on toast
Chocolate mousse
Summer fruits
White wine
Iced tea and iced coffee

[2]
A Winter Tea

Onion tart squares
Crostini (mozzarella cheese and anchovies on Italian bread, baked and napped with garlic-flavored melted butter) cut into bite-sized pieces
Sandwiches (on homemade white bread or brioche rounds):
Foie gras
Salmon mousse
Cucumber
Rare roast beef with mustard sauce
Hot tea or coffee   Hot rum punch or mulled cider

The Rehearsal Dinner

Since the number of guests is not generally very large, rehearsal dinners are almost always seated. They may be as simple or elaborate, as formal or as informal as you wish. Although the groom's family frequently gives the dinner, the bride is consulted and often makes many of the arrangements herself if her future in-laws are from another city. Cocktails may be served first, and wine or champagne is appropriate with all the meals.

Least Formal

Antipasto of salamis, prosciutto, mussels, anchovies, vegetables
Moussaka
Rice with pine nuts
Green salad
Small cream puffs
Red wine   Coffee and tea

[2]
More Formal

Mussels with a rémoulade sauce
Sautéed chicken with artichoke hearts
Fresh noodles
Purée of carrots
Green salad
French bread
Open orange tart
White wine   Coffee

[3]
Most Formal

Seviche (raw marinated fish)
Consommé
Duck with apples
Crisp sautéed vegetables
Shoestring potatoes
Orange sherbert in orange shells   Cookies
Red wine   Coffee

15

THE MOST-ASKED WEDDING QUESTIONS

The questions in this chapter have been selected from those most frequently asked by my readers. For easy reference they are divided into the following categories: Finances, Engagements, Choosing Attendants, Clothing, Invitations and Announcements, Prewedding Events, Reception, Gifts, Second Marriages, General Questions.

Finances

Q. What expenses do the bride and her family pay?

A. When the bride's family is giving the wedding, they pay for the invitations, announcements, wedding and reception expenses, the bride's bouquet (where customary), flowers for the bride's attendants, the bridegroom's ring, a present for the groom if the bride wishes, presents for the bridesmaids, and church fees other than the donation to the minister.

Q. What expenses does a groom have?

A. The wedding ring, the marriage license, a present for his bride, presents for his best man and his ushers, ties, gloves, and boutonnieres for his attendants, the clergyman's fee, the bride's bouquet (this depends on local custom), the bride's corsage, corsages for the mothers, and all expenses of the honeymoon.

Q. What expenses do the attendants have?

A. They pay for their own clothes, either rented or purchased. They usually give a joint present to the bride or groom, as well as a personal gift. Attendants pay for their own transportation to the site of the wedding, but the bride or groom is responsible for their lodging. The bridesmaids often give a shower for the bride.

Q. Who pays for the lodging expenses for the groom's family or friends when they come from out of town?

A. They pay their own expenses if staying at a motel or hotel. However, the bride's family should do their best to arrange to have them stay at a relative's or friend's home.

Q. Does the groom's family ever pay any of the costs of the reception?

A. Yes. For certain ethnic groups, it is customary for the groom's family to pay for the liquor or for the hall. Also, when the groom's family (and the bride and groom) want a more elaborate reception than the bride's parents can afford, the groom's family may *offer* to help out, in order to accommodate a larger number. However, they should abide by the bride's parents' wishes, and not insist, if there is any resentment.

Engagements

Q. When a couple becomes engaged, which family makes the first move to meet the other?

A. Traditionally the groom's. They used to "call on" the bride's family; today they usually telephone and arrange a meeting at their own home or however they wish. If they live in different towns, the groom's mother writes a letter immediately; and as soon as possible, whichever family can travel more conveniently visits the other. If the groom's family is unaware of this convention, however, the bride's family should step in and make the first call, rather than let the situation become uncomfortable.

Q. May an engagement be announced before the groom gives the bride a ring?

A. Yes. It is not necessary to have a ring to become engaged, and many couples prefer to wait until the man can afford exactly the ring he wants for his bride.

Q. How is an engagement announced?

A. It is announced by word of mouth, by personal note, by a newspaper announcement, and often by a party. Engraved announcements are not sent out.

Q. When is the engagement party held, and who attends?

A. The party is given by the bride's parents and is usually held at the same time the news is made public. It may be a very small dinner for only the two families, or it may be a large reception including all the relatives and close friends of the couple. Guests do not need to bring gifts, as only people very close to the bride give engagement presents.

Q. When a man's fiancée lives in another city, may his parents give an engagement party to introduce her to their friends?

A. Yes, but it should take place after the announcement and after any party the bride's family might give in their city. In other words, it is the privilege of the bride's family to make the first announcement and celebration.

Choosing Attendants

Q. What are the age limits for flower girls, ring bearers, junior ushers, and junior bridesmaids?

A. Flower girls, 3 to 7; ring bearers, 3 to 7; junior ushers and bridesmaids, 8 to 14.

Q. Is there any rule about the number of ushers and bridesmaids?

A. Yes. The general rule of thumb is one usher for every fifty guests. There are frequently, therefore, more ushers than bridesmaids at a large wedding, but there should never be more bridesmaids than ushers.

Q. Is it obligatory for the bride to have the groom's sisters as attendants?

A. It is not obligatory, especially if she does not know them. But if they are close to her age, it is a very nice gesture and helps the bride to create a happy relationship with her new family.

Q. Who escorts the bride if she has no father?

A. An older brother, an uncle, or a godfather are first choices. If she has no relatives or godparents, a close family friend may serve. A foreigner, or a girl from far away, whose marriage will take place in the groom's hometown, sometimes asks her groom's father to escort her. In each case, the bride's mother if she is present, rather than the escort, responds "I do" when the minister asks "Who giveth this woman?" In fact, in this day of one-parent families, more and more brides are asking if their mother may escort them. I see no objection, if there is no male relative or friend close enough to assume this duty. The bride may also walk unescorted if she wishes.

Clothing

Q. Should the bride's mother and the groom's mother wear the same length and style of dress?

A. Since they will stand together in the receiving line, it will make a more pleasing picture if the groom's mother elects to wear a dress similar in type to the one being worn by the bride's mother. It is the bride's mother, however, who chooses the style and then lets the groom's mother know what she has selected.

Q. Do men wear dinner jackets (tuxedos) at all formal weddings?

A. No. Tuxedos are not correct in the daytime and should be worn only at an evening wedding—one taking place after five o'clock. For daytime formal wear, men wear cutaways (most formal) or striped trousers with sack coats (less formal).

Q. I have a three-year-old son born out of wedlock. May I wear a white wedding gown at my forthcoming marriage?

A. You may wear whatever gown would make you happiest; but you should not wear a veil, unless your religion requires it, nor should you carry orange blossoms as your bouquet.

Q. Does the mother of the bride (or groom) wear a coat as she walks up the aisle in cold weather?

A. She might wear a jacket, cape or stole that would complement her dress. But other coats would hide her carefully chosen costume, and it is better to have one of the ushers put a coat in her pew ahead of time, which she may put over her shoulders during the ceremony.

Q. Do flower girls wear the same style dress as the bridesmaids?

A. Not necessarily. The color should be the same, or blend with the bridesmaids' dresses. But while the style should be similar, it should be adapted to be becoming to a child. The flower girl may also wear white if the bride prefers.

Q. When the groom is a serviceman, should he wear his uniform?

A. If our nation is not officially at war, military regulations ordinarily allow a member of the armed forces to choose whether or not to wear his uniform when off base or off duty. Usually his decision will depend on his bride's wishes. In the event he elects to wear his uniform, then those of his ushers who are in service should also wear theirs. If both bride and groom are in the service, the bride may also choose to wear her uniform. However, if she is marrying a civilian she should wear a traditional wedding gown.

Invitations and Announcements

Q. How far in advance of the wedding are invitations sent?

A. Four to six weeks beforehand for a large wedding or up to ten days before for a simpler wedding.

Q. Is it in good taste to enclose reply cards with invitations to a wedding reception?

A. It is an honor to be invited to a wedding, and the least that one can do is to answer the invitation promptly by hand. Unfortunately, many people do not appreciate the honor, and the use of answer cards is sometimes the only way to determine accurately how many people can be expected to attend. If you feel this is the case in your area, you are justified in using them.

Q. How can one tell invitees that their children are *not* included?

A. If you are afraid that your guests will bring their children even though the address in the envelope does not include their names, the best solution is to explain to your relatives and friends that you are terribly sorry but you cannot include children. Ask them to help you by spreading the word. It is not correct to print "Please do not bring children" or similar words on an invitation.

Q. When the bride's parents are divorced and both have remarried, is it proper to include all four names on the invitations?

A. Invitations should be issued in the name of the couple who pays for and acts as host at the wedding and reception. Only in the event that relations are so friendly that both couples share the expenses and act as cohosts should all four names appear.

Q. Should invitations be sent to relatives and friends living too far away to attend the wedding?

A. This really depends on the closeness of your relationship with them. Since receiving an invitation to a reception customarily requires that one send a gift, many people prefer to send announcements instead, for they carry no obligation. However, very close friends—who would wish to send a gift in any case—would be hurt if they received only an announcement, so they should be included on the invitation list, even though they cannot attend.

Q. How soon after a wedding are announcements sent?

A. The sooner the better, so that friends living out of town will receive the news as quickly as possible. However, there is no strict limitation, and announcements of an elopement or a secret marriage may be sent as long as a year after the wedding.

Q. Why aren't the names of the groom's mother and father included on the wedding invitation?

A. When the wedding and reception are given by the bride's family, the invitations are issued in their name. Only in the event that the groom's family are also hosts, and assume a full share of the expenses, do their names appear.

Q. Should invitations be sent to the groom's parents and the attendents?

A. Yes. They need not answer them, but they enjoy having them as mementos.

Q. Just when may a wedding invitation be addressed to "Mr. and Mrs. John Smith and Family"?

Q. It is always preferable, if possible, to send individual invitations, or write a young child's name below that of his or her parents. However, if you are limited as to number of invitations, or you do not know the names of the children, you may use "and family." When you do, it means that *every* member living at that address is invited.

Q. How is the total number of invitations divided between the bride's family and the groom's?

A. They should be divided evenly. If the groom lives far away and cannot use his share, his mother should tell the bride's mother how many of her invitations will be unused and therefore available to the bride's "side."

Q. Is it correct to invite co-workers in your office to your wedding with a single invitation posted on the bulletin board?

A. It is permissible, but remember that it means that everyone, *and* their husbands and wives, are invited. If you can afford the extra invitations, it is preferable to send them individually.

Prewedding Events

Q. Who gives bridal showers, and how many may a bride have?

A. Bridal attendants, family friends, and relatives may and do give showers. Members of the immediate family—mothers and sisters of the bride or groom—should not do so. There is no specific rule about the number of showers, but it is an imposition to ask friends to go to several and bring a gift to each. The bride should go over the guest lists with the hostesses and divide them up so that no one person is invited to more than one or, at the most, two showers.

Q. Are showers for women only?

A. No indeed. Showers that include the groom and male guests are often held in the evening. Bottle or bar showers, workshop showers, garden showers—all are appropriate.

Q. Must a bride write thank-you notes for shower presents?

A. Only to those guests who are not present. If she personally and warmly thanks each friend for her gift as it is opened, she need do no more.

Q. What is the bridesmaids' luncheon?

A. It may be a luncheon given by the bride for the bridesmaids or vice versa. It is exactly like any other women's luncheon except that the decorations are a little more elaborate and "bridey," and the bride may be given a corsage. The bridesmaids usually give the bride their joint present at that time, and the bride may present her gifts to them.

Q. Who gives the rehearsal dinner and who attends it?

A. The groom's parents usually give the dinner, although it is not obligatory. If they live in another area, they may ask the bride's mother to reserve a place for the dinner and make the preliminary arrangements. They make final arrangements when they arrive for the wedding, and, of course, they pay the expenses. Otherwise a member of the bride's family or a close friend may give the dinner. The bridal party, immediate families of the bride and groom, and, if possible, out-of-town friends who arrive the day before the wedding make up the list. The clergyman, if he is a family friend, is often included. Wives, husbands, and fiancé(e)s of the attendants also are invited.

Q. What is a "bachelor's dinner?"

A. It is a party for the groom and his attendants held a week or so before the wedding and given either by the ushers or the groom's father. Traditionally it was a wild party to mark the end of the groom's bachelorhood, but more often it is just a get-together with good food, good drinks, good friends, some jokes, and some reminiscences.

Reception

Q. Do the fathers of both bride and groom stand in the receiving line?

A. They usually do, but it is not obligatory. They may be happier, and more useful, circulating among the guests.

Q. When is the wedding cake cut, and what is the procedure?

A. At a seated dinner the cake is usually cut after the main course is eaten, and it is served as part of the dessert. When the meal is a buffet, or there is no bridal table, the cake is cut just before the couple leaves to change out of wedding clothes. In both cases, the bride, with the groom helping by placing his hand over hers on the knife, cuts the first two slices. He feeds her the first bite, and she offers him the second. The rest of the cake is cut and served by the waiters, or, at a very small wedding, by members of the family.

Q. What is the order for dancing at the reception?

A. The bride and groom always dance the first dance together. The groom's father usually cuts in, and the groom asks the bride's mother to dance. The bride's father dances with her next, her father-in-law cuts in on her mother, and the groom asks his own mother to dance. The precise order is not important so long as each of the principal men dances with the bride and the mothers first. The dancing, after that, becomes general.

Q. Who sits at the parents' table and where do husbands, wives, and fiancé(e)s of attendants sit at a seated reception?

A. The parents of *both* bride and groom, the clergyman and his or her spouse, if any, and, according to space, grandparents, godparents, and close relatives. The spouses and fiancé(e)s of married attendants should be included at the bridal table. If that is impossible because of space, they join other friends, but the married attendants must stay with the bridal party.

Gifts

Q. How should checks given as wedding presents be made out?

A. When given before the wedding they are made out either to the bride, Katherine Adams, or to both bride and groom, Katherine Adams and Brian Jamison. When given after the wedding they are made out to Katherine and Brian Jamison. (Members of either family may, however, make the check out to their son or daughter alone if they prefer.)

Q. May duplicate wedding presents be exchanged?

A. Yes. Whether you tell the donor or not depends on whether they are close enough to you so they might notice the absence of their original gift.

Q. When the presents are displayed, should cards showing the names of the donors be displayed with them?

A. This is a matter of personal preference. Although many people like to know who gave what present, others feel that publicizing this information invites comparisons that may be embarrassing.

Q. How should checks which are displayed with wedding presents be shown?

A. They should be arranged overlapping, so that the signature but not the amount shows. Cover them with a piece of glass to keep them in place.

Q. When a wedding gift arrives broken, what should a bride do?

A. Take it back to the store from which it came, without mentioning the fact to the donor. If it has arrived directly through the mail, however, the donor should be notified so that he or she can collect insurance.

Q. Are printed thank-you cards an acceptable way of acknowledging wedding presents?

A. Only if a personal message is added. The truly correct thank you is a personal handwritten note, which is most appropriately written on the bride's own stationery. (One exception is a thank-you card incorporating the bridal couple's wedding picture, but this, too, must always include a personal handwritten message.)

Q. Should wedding presents be opened at the reception?

A. At a small wedding where there are only a few, they may be opened, but if there are many presents, it is better to wait until later so that the bride and groom may mingle with the guests. The couple will also appreciate the gifts more if they open them at their leisure.

Second Marriages

Q. Should children of a first marriage be present at a parent's second marriage?

A. Unless they are bitter, or dislike the second husband or wife, they should definitely attend. Nothing could serve better to make them feel a part of the excitement and help them to accept a new family relationship.

Q. May a woman have a shower before her second marriage?

A. Yes, but it should be a small and intimate party, since a bride should not expect many gifts at her second marriage.

Q. What does a widow do with her first engagement and wedding ring when she remarries?

A. When she becomes engaged she ceases wearing them, although, if she has children, she may wish to wear her wedding ring until her marriage. Her first engagement ring may be kept for her children, or the stone may be reset in another piece of jewelry.

Q. What are the rules about clothing for a bride who is being married for the second time?

A. She may not wear any emblem of virginity such as a bridal veil, orange blossoms, or a myrtle wreath. Pale colors or off-white are preferable to pure white, although white is acceptable when worn with colored accessories.

Q. Is it correct to send engraved invitations to a second marriage?

A. Yes, invitations to a large wedding and reception may be exactly like those for a first marriage, except that the bride's whole name is used.

General Questions

Q. Do the friends of the bride always sit on one side of the church and the friends of the groom on the other?

A. The left side is traditionally the bride's side, and the right is the groom's. However, ushers should try to keep the number of guests on both sides of the aisle as balanced as possible. If a great majority of the guests are friends of one or the other, an usher may say to a guest, "Would you mind sitting on Michael's side? There are better seats there."

Q. Does the bride walk up the aisle on her father's right arm or left arm?

A. On his right arm. This is traditionally correct and has the added advantage of leaving him in the most convenient position to reach his seat in the left front pew afterward. It also leaves the bride's right arm free to be given to the groom, who will join her from the right.

Q. How are divorced parents seated in the church?

A. The bride's mother (and stepfather) sit in the front pew. The bride's father (after giving her away in a Protestant ceremony) sits behind them with his second wife, as long as she is friendly with the bride. The same procedure is followed by the groom's family.

Q. What part do grandparents have in a wedding?

A. They are merely honored guests. They sit in the second pew and they are seated at the parents' table at the reception. They do not stand in the receiving line, and they have no duties other than to enjoy the occasion.

Q. May a couple who have been living together for some time have a church wedding and a reception?

A. Yes, indeed. Their decision to marry is a happy one, and the occasion should be celebrated with as much sincerity and rejoicing as any other wedding.

About the Author

Elizabeth L. Post, granddaughter-in-law of the legendary Emily Post, has earned the mantle of her predecessor as America's foremost authority on etiquette. Mrs. Post has revised the classic *Etiquette* four times since 1965 and is now at work on another revision to be published in 1992. In addition she has written *Emily Post's Wedding Planner; Emily Post on Business Etiquette; Emily Post on Entertaining; Emily Post on Etiquette; Emily Post on Invitations and Letters; Emily Post on Second Weddings; Emily Post on Weddings; Please, Say Please; The Complete Book of Entertaining* with co-author Anthony Staffieri, and *Emily Post Talks with Teens About Manners and Etiquette* with co-author Joan M. Coles. Mrs. Post's advice on etiquette may also be found in the monthly column she writes for *Good Housekeeping* magazine, "Etiquette for Everyday."

Mrs. Post and her husband divide their time between homes in Florida and Vermont.